Working with Young People in Loss Situations

CW00550636

LONGMAN

Author: LINDA MACHIN

Artist: WESTON SAMUELS

Working with Young People in Loss Situations

Author: Linda Machin   Artist: Weston Samuels

Published by Longman Information and Reference
Longman Group UK Ltd, 6th Floor, Westgate House, The High,
Harlow, Essex CM20 1YR, England.

A catalogue record for this manual is available from the British Library.

ISBN 0-582-21622-2

Typeset and printed by How & Blackhall, Berwick-upon-Tweed (0289) 307553.
Design/Editing: Alan Dearling.

CONTENTS

Acknowledgements.   1

Introduction.   2

PART 1

Guidelines and instructions for the use of pictures contained in the manual.   3

A counselling approach to help children and young people cope with loss.   9

PART 2

Situations of loss in childhood: 13
    1. Lost and damaging relationships   13
    2. Physical and intellectual development   14
    3. Economic disadvantage   14
    4. Unfulfilled ambitions.   15

The context of loss: 16
    1. Home   16
    2. School   17
    3. Informal social groups.   18

Childhood attachment.   18

Grief — the Response to loss: 19
    1. Denial   20
    2. Emotional anguish   20
    3. Partial adjustment   21
    4. Acceptance.   22

How adults understand grief and the implications for grieving children and young people.   23

Symptoms of grief in children and young people.   25

Bibliography   **28**

PART 3

Picture Resources: 29

SHEET NUMBERS

A: Picture story lines. (A) 1 to 5   30-34

B: Picture situations. (B) 6-9   35-38

C: Individual trigger pictures. (C) 10-42   39-52

D: Worksheets 1-35   72-106

Suggested work programmes.   107

CONTENTS

Acknowledgements ... 1

Introduction ... 2

PART 1

Guidelines and instructions for the use of pictures contained in the manual ... 5

A counselling approach to help children and young people cope with loss ... 6

PART 2

Significance of loss in childhood ... 13
1. Loss and damaging relationships ... 13
2. Physical and intellectual development ... 14
3. Economic disadvantage ... 14
4. Unfulfilled ambitions ... 15

The context of loss ... 15
1. Home ... 16
2. School ... 17
3. Informal social groups ... 18

Childhood structures ... 19
Children belonging to loss ... 19
1. Denial ... 20
2. Emotional anxiety ... 22
3. 21
4. Acceptance ... 22

How suffering ... and the implications for grieving children and young people ... 23

Symptoms of grief in children and young people ... 24

Challenging ... 26

PART 3

Picture Resources ... 29

SHEET NUMBERS

A. Picture story lines (A) 1 to 5 ... 30-34
B. Picture situations (B) 6-9 ... 35-38
C. Individual trigger cards (C) 10-12 ... 39-52
D. Worksheets 14-58 ... 72-106

Suggested work programme ... 107

ACKNOWLEDGEMENTS

I would like to thank especially those young clients who, while gaining support in their grief, have taught me so much about the child's experience of loss and done so with trust and courage. Bereavement Care, the counselling and training organisation which I founded in North Staffordshire in 1984, has been the context of the help and learning, and I would like to thank all those staff members and volunteers who have used their skill over the years in caring for the bereaved and in maintaining quality support for the counsellors within that organisation.

The process of developing this material owes much to the help and insight of other people, including Pat Mood, Elizabeth Dunn, Olive Otway, the pupils of St Luke's Primary School, Hanley, Wood Lane Primary School and Madeley High School, Staffordshire.

Thanks also must go to the television Telethon Appeal who have provided funding for this work to be taken forward. The guidance of Alan Dearling, Commissioning Publisher, has been important in suggesting revisions that will allow the material to be more accessible to a wider practitioner group. To Weston Samuels, artist, my thanks are due for the many hours of discussion and drawing, which were part of the lengthy process of designing picture material for entering a childhood experience of loss.

Working with Young People in Loss Situations

INTRODUCTION

As Director of Bereavement Care in North Staffordshire (1984-90), I became increasingly convinced of the importance of looking at the needs of bereaved children. Sometimes, referrals would be made for counselling help for a child, but more often those needs would be seen through the eyes of a parent, who was using the counselling services of Bereavement Care. At other times our awareness of the needs of a grieving child would be raised through the concern of a professional carer who was seeking guidance for a young bereaved person.

The need to offer an appropriate and direct service to children is twofold; first to meet current bereavement distress at the point of need, and secondly, in so doing, to help alleviate the long-term ill effects of bereavement. It is important to understand that grief is as powerful and distressing for children as it is for adults, but that the manifestations of the grief and the manner of working with it is different.

I have already used pictures as a potential educational method for exploring the world of loss, Machin and Holt (1988) and felt that pictures would also provide a useful tool for counselling children. A pilot was undertaken with a counselling colleague and it proved successful as a way of helping children. The idea has been taken further, and this current publication aims not only to provide a resource for those working with bereaved children, but also for anyone doing direct work with children who have suffered a loss.

All adults have been children and yet as adults we can be daunted when faced with the distress of children. The desire to protect them from premature exposure to emotional pain, and a tendency to retreat from memories of painful events in our own childhood, often result in a gulf of silence. Such silence and avoidance serves children badly as they struggle to accommodate the pains of loss and change.

This manual explores grief in children and provides a resource which can enable adult carers, whether those undertaking therapeutic work or those who are professionally or voluntarily in contact with children and young people, to enter that world of grief and support the child through the process of resolving the pain.

The manual is divided into three parts: —

Part 1. Contains suggestions and guidance for using the picture material with grieving children. It also outlines a counselling approach, which offers a sensitive and practical framework for addressing the grief of children and young people.

Part 2. Provides information designed to give insight into the experience of loss in childhood; the range of experiences, the context of experience, the processes of human attachment and grief, how adults understand (misunderstand) children's grief and the symptoms of grief in childhood.

'Grief' is the term used throughout this material to refer to the collective, emotional, physical and social responses to loss situations.

The picture resources are the core of the manual, and are contained in **Part 3.** Their use is explained fully in Part 1 of the manual which follows.

Part 1

GUIDELINES AND INSTRUCTIONS FOR THE USE OF THE PICTURES CONTAINED IN THIS MANUAL

At the heart of working directly with children, who are grieving because of either a temporary or permanent loss, is the need for them to focus on their 'story' consisting of events, people, feelings and perceptions. An important route into this complex world of experience can be through visual images. This manual uses a number of visual methods to access the 'story'. The range of visual material provided in Part 3 of the manual includes:

(A) Story Lines
(B) Picture Situations
(C) Trigger Pictures
(D) Work Sheets

To each picture and situation, dialogue and thoughts can be added. Individual pictures explore a wide range of loss situations, and pictures can be incorporated into work sheets. These along with the insights contained in Parts 1 and 2 of this manual offer the potential for a supportive response to a child or young person who is coping with loss.

Picture material contained in Part 3 of this manual

A. Storylines

These are a set of 5 **story lines** depicting a range of childhood encounters with loss.

> A.1 **Getting lost**
> A.2 **Losing a gift**
> A.3 **Death of a pet**
> A.4 **Being ill**
> A.5 **Moving to another 'home'**

All of these allow for children to identify events and the feelings which go with them. Some will relate objectively to circumstances which they have not experienced, but for others it will link directly with events which are real for them. The 'Moving to another ''home'' story line will be particularly relevant for those children whose domestic circumstances demand that either formal, or informal, arrangements have had to be made for them to move out of their home situation.

To use the story line pictures, photocopy them for use with the child and select the one which is relevant to the focus of your work. If you plan to work with more than one story line, begin with the least threatening. Allow the child to feel safe with you and with the materials. For example, 'getting lost' and 'losing a gift' might afford a more general exploration of events and feelings before addressing the loss for which this child is grieving currently.

Invite the young person to study the pictures and either:

1. Tell you a story about what they think is happening, OR

2. Write a caption below each picture to say what is happening.

Then invite the child to say whether they have experienced anything similar to the 'story'. Use prompts such as:

''Does the story remind you of anything which has happened to you?''

''What did you feel about the event?''

''Were you able to talk about it to anyone?''

''What do you feel now as you remember that event?''

Some children might enjoy creating their own story sequence either from photographs or drawings or a mixture of both. See worksheet 34 for a blank format which may be used.

B. Picture situations.

This is a development in the story line approach using **picture situations** that might link with adolescent experience, but may also be used with younger children. The approach allows for something more than simple story telling, using thought and speech bubbles to explore further what might be going on for the people in the pictures.

B.6	**Illness**
B.7	**Unemployment**
B.8	**Relationships**
B.9	**Money**

Photocopy the pictures and choose the one(s) which help focus on the situations and feelings which are appropriate to the help being offered.

1. Invite the young person to study the picture sequence and fill in the speech and thought bubbles.
If the space provided is insufficient then ask them to write, outside the pictures, what they imagine the people might be thinking and saying.

2. Ask them to write or tell what they think is happening in the story sequence.

3. Ask them to describe any similar situation which they have experienced.

This is an opportunity for the young person to be much more specific, and they may need some help in exploring events which were painful or confusing. Prompts about, what happened, who else was involved, what it felt like and what are the feelings in recalling these events, can be given to facilitate the telling of the child's own story. Children are likely to resist if they feel that the prompts have become uncomfortable probes, but carers need to be alert for signs that a child, especially one who is anxious to please, is not being pushed into disclosures which increase their vulnerability.

If you are uncertain, always check:

"Do you want to stop now?"

"Is this difficult or do you want to continue?"

Such checking helps ensure that the child has freedom of choice, a factor which may have been absent from other relationships with adults. Where wider or deeper explorations are desirable/possible, then the pictures themselves can engender a deeper focus. For example:

B.6 may be used to address illness in the family or conflicting responsibilities.

B.7 looks at issues of unemployment but may also focus on a young person's encounter with authority.

B.8 explores interpersonal relationships and also may help address more specifically, conflicts between generations and gender issues in the family.

B.9 in looking at money could also explore at a deeper level honesty, poverty, and problems for young people in a consumer society.

Some young people may not focus instantly on the less immediate subject of the picture and the teacher/parent/carer may have to identify those issues, to further the discussion.

C. Trigger pictures

Single **trigger pictures** are used in this section; they explore a wide range of contexts in which children might (a) encounter loss, (b) situations which engender powerful emotions, and (c) scenarios which depict behaviour which is a manifestation of emotion.

C.10/11/12	General scenarios carrying some implied loss
C.13/14/15	Encounters with authority
C.16/17/18/19/20	Situations related to illness and disability
C.21/22/23/24/25/26/27/28/29	Relationship scenarios
C.30/31/32	Youth focused scenarios
C.33/34	Bereavement
C.35/36/37/38/39/40/41/42	Scenarios with a feeling component but where the situation need to be elaborated in the context of the child/young person's own experience.

There are a variety of ways in which these can be used:

1. Allow the child to choose four or five pictures to tell a story. It is unwieldy to give them a choice from a range of more than twelve. Your selection should be based initially on the telling of a fairly neutral story. At this stage the story may not focus on their loss. This approach will help familiarise the child with the medium of the pictures as a 'trigger' for discussion. You can assist that discussion by looking at how the picture sequence has connected events, what feelings are associated with the events, and what relationship issues might emerge.

2. Allow the child to choose a picture (from not more than a range of twelve) to say something about their own experience. At this stage, the range you choose may well reflect some awareness of the child's experience of loss but it will increase your insight, and that of the child, as they describe their emotional responses to significant events.

3. Select a number of pictures and ask the child to describe each of them. Build up a sequence that is significant for the child. The selection is likely to be based on a fairly clear knowledge of the child's general experience, or, as a way of addressing the specific loss currently being grieved. Used in this way the pictures will highlight painful experience, and these painful feelings may be overtly expressed or covertly felt. Being sensitive to the pace and depth at which the child can work comfortably, is an important task for the carer. Such sensitivity may come from observing the child's distressed reactions, but also in asking the child at stages during the work, how the process is feeling and whether they need to pause for a while. It is essential to distinguish between that distress which arises naturally from the recall of painful events and that which is created by an intrusive style of 'helping'. Reassuring children about the normality of their feelings, and of the benefits of sharing difficult experiences, must not rob them of the freedom to choose to disclose to someone else, to disclose on another occasion, or to vary the pace of their disclosure.

4. Select individual pictures for the child's response. This may be one way of maintaining a slower pace or of working at more depth, especially if one of the pictures is a very direct reflection of the situation which the child is grieving.

5. Include individual pictures into worksheets — see D.33. This can then incorporate other styles of disclosure, e.g. writing and drawing. For many children this may allow for a safer and more controlled communication of events and feelings than occurs when in dialogue with a 'powerful' adult.

D. Work Sheets.

These are a set of **work sheets** designed to enable children as individuals or in groups, make written as well as verbal responses to the material. The emphasis is on giving children a greater opportunity to reflect upon, and appraise experience not merely to describe it. Young children or those uncomfortable with writing should be encouraged to draw their own pictures. For others, drawing can be seen as a powerful alternative to the spoken or written word. This provides very rich material for discussion and exploration.

Some flexibility is built into this section for users to choose pictures from other parts of the pack which focus upon themes appropriate to the style and level of the work being undertaken, for instance D.33.

In selecting an appropriate range of pictures it can be helpful to move from the general (worksheets containing more straightforwardly descriptive exercises: i.e. D.1,2,3,4,5,6) to the more specific (worksheets with pictures that invite a very particular focus: i.e. D.10,17,19).

1. Photocopy the worksheet for use by the child/young person.
2. Read the instructions to or with the child, making sure that they understand what is being asked.
3. Provide appropriate materials, pens, pencils, paints, etc. and if necessary help the child choose the medium they would most like to use.
4. Give time and appropriate working space for the child to complete the task. Stay with the child as they work; observing and showing interest, but not asking questions or interpreting what is being done. This is an important part of demonstrating to the child that they are valued, and that they are building up a 'real' relationship. Often adults ask children to write or draw when they are not available, or do not choose to be free, to give them attention. In this situation the attention of the teacher/parent/carer is an important, if apparently passive, part of the process of enabling the child to process painful experience.
5. When the worksheet exercise is complete, ask the child to tell you about it; giving an opportunity to explain what has already been committed to paper and how in explaining it, facts and feelings can be elaborated.

In some of the worksheet responses a direct connection will be evident between experiences and feelings, e.g. D.7,8,9,10, but within others it may not be so obvious, e.g. D.29,30,31,32. In these last examples, it is important for the carer/counsellor to probe gently enough to be able to gauge the child's capacity to explore the feelings, or to decide whether the expression of them in cryptic form is a sign of defence mechanisms working. For example, in worksheet D.29 there may be an apparent connection between this 'fantasy' drawing and real people who pose threats. The child should be helped to move at a pace, which is safe for them from the imaginary aspects of the picture and on to the relationships and experiences which are being echoed in the picture. Defence mechanisms have offered protection in the past and should not be overridden ahead of the child's own ability to confront painful realities in their world. In worksheet D.32 you may want to look at whether there are themes within the shapes that the child observes within their picture. E.g. Are they neutral images, happy images or frightening images? This may give a guide as to the overall mood of the child.

Throughout Worksheet section D. try to recognise (a) the 'story' telling element, which may include new and painful disclosures, (b) the opportunity it affords to identify and give expression to feelings, and (c) the part it might play in looking at new or different strategies for handling loss and change.

6. Discuss whether the child is to take the worksheet home, or whether it is to be kept by the carer (or copies made so that both can be possible). This is part of the process of giving choice, and valuing the child's painful experience and their processing of it.

Situations in which pictures might be used in working with children

It is assumed that users of these pictures will already possess communication and intervention skills gained through training and/or experience, in some aspect of work with young people. It may be that the pictures supplement other working methods such as family therapy, counselling, etc., or it may be that this is going to be the main method used in a teaching, social work or residential context. Whether the pictures are a primary or secondary focus should determine the selection of picture themes. Where it is **secondary**, the choice of pictures will be most effective if they complement the therapeutic style, by affording another method of focusing on the child's concerns, e.g. the child who is looking at relationships in family therapy may, on an individual basis, benefit from pursuing similar themes in the pictures. Where the pictures are the **primary** working method, the therapist will devise most profitably a systematic programme that is appropriate for an individual child. For example:

1. Background pictures of situations that will be 'safe' at the beginning of a relationship with a child.
2. Moving on to scenarios that relate to the child's experience.
3. At a later stage using the pictures which rouse or invite a deeper exploration of feelings.

Flexibility is always important. Younger children whose concentration span is limited, are likely to want to look at more pictures and spend less time on each.

Work in groups

Help which is offered in school, social work or residential context may use the pictures and worksheets as a group activity. This may be appropriate either where the group needs to resolve:

(a) Loss experienced collectively, e.g. death of a school friend.

(b) Loss involved with admission into residential care or moving from home to a residential school setting, i.e. a common loss for all individuals in the group.

(c) Where the themes of loss are part of a programme of social and life skills.

Where there is a collective and immediate group loss, facilitators (leaders/teachers, etc.) will have to address several dimensions of grief; individual, sub-group (e.g. immediate friendship group of a child killed in a road traffic accident), wider community. If leaders are part of the 'grieving community', they will have personal feelings to work through at a time when young people are especially needing their supportive leadership. Where there is a community tragedy, such as the Hillsborough football disaster, King's Cross fire, etc., counsellors/carers are particularly vulnerable to the trauma of listening to repeated accounts of horrific events. Support for counsellors in this situation is crucial and appropriate breaks from the intensity of absorbing high levels of distress are essential. This is a particularly intense counselling situation and individual tragedy and loss will be demanding upon carers. Support and supervision are a necessary element of the resources required for the work of caring for children and young people.

One important way of establishing support for the leader, in the group context, is by working out a leadership strategy in which two or more adults plan, lead and debrief their sessions. Leaders could work most effectively jointly on choosing pictures and worksheets which help the group to look at events and feelings. The planning should include deciding when and where to meet and whether the membership is open (for anyone in a class) or closed (for smaller chosen or self-selected sub-groups within a class).

Having formed the group, the leader's task is to make 'ground rules' within the group to ensure that there is a common understanding about confidentiality. For instance people should not be under any obligation to disclose more than is comfortable/appropriate for them, and it should be clear whether individual help is available, outside the group, for people who need additional support. When the leaders are sure that all group members are comfortable with the basis on which the work is to be undertaken, then the task can begin.

The working method of looking at loss through the medium of pictures is then explained and any uncertainties clarified. At this stage, individuals can be asked to look at the picture material and share in pairs their responses to the visual images. Young people should be reminded that they share only the material and the feelings that feel safe for them. Having given time for this (appropriate time will depend on the age of the group and their capacity to reflect on the exercise) the group as a whole can look at the elements which are common. This gives an opportunity to work at a personal level and to make supportive connections with peers.

Leaders will need to be alert for individuals who are exploring particularly painful issues and also facilitate dialogue within the group. This aspect of leadership — passively registering individual reactions and enabling the group to be an active forum for discussion — is especially effective when two people share these functions. A reflection on the dynamics will be part of the debriefing process. Understanding what has been happening within the group will help inform the planning of subsequent sessions. When the work of the group has come to an end it is important to review what has been achieved.

It is necessary to distinguish between the **therapeutic** use and **educational** use of this pack. It is therapeutic where it assists with an immediate personal grief, and educational where it has a more objective purpose for exploring grief in a group context. Whatever the primary purpose of the pictures, therapeutic or educational, it should be remembered that the pictures may act as an emotional trigger even in those situations which seem to carry less immediate personal grief. Whether working with individual children or groups, facilitators should plan a thematic use of the pictures appropriate to the purposes of their work.

Individual work

The pictures provide a way of working with a child at the point of their experience and of facilitating communication. It is not a tool of psychological interpretation. The child or young person should be given an explanation of what is intended — working methods; whether the pictures stand alone or are part of other kinds of counselling help. Children will vary in their willingness to talk with adults and this in itself may reflect the grief they are feeling.

Clarity about confidentiality needs to be given. Distinguishing between those disclosures, which in the interests of the child's own safety cannot be confidential; those which may need to be discussed with the child as a prelude to the carer and child sharing knowledge with other appropriate people and those which can remain in the therapeutic context between child, carer, and supervisor. The concept of supervision will be a familiar one to professional therapists and counsellors. All carers will find it important to obtain support from another person, who understands the nature and the context of the help being offered, as an essential safeguard both for the carer and the person being helped.

As the child or young person begins to respond to the pictures, minimum interventions should be made by the adult facilitator. In this way, the immediacy of the stimulus will be unaffected by the sense of giving a 'right' response. General prompts such as ''tell me more about that'', ''what do you think the people in the picture were feeling?'', ''what might you be feeling?'' — will ease the process of communication without determining what the child might say.

Hearing what is said, observing non-verbal messages, and staying alert to topics which are resisted, are all important tasks for the facilitator. Awareness gained from accurate attention to the child's 'messages' will assist in deciding the stage and pace at which the child can tolerate confrontation with central aspects of their loss. Allowing the child or young person to move into details of their experience, and be heard and accepted, is a crucial therapeutic element to follow from the earlier neutral descriptions of loss, which they have seen contained in the pictures.

The facilitator's existing experience with children or young people, may not have prepared them for the expression of feelings which may result from working with these pictures. It is necessary to recognise that tears and anger are not indications of weakness or emotional breakdown, but are important ways of getting rid of pent-up emotion. A period of peacefulness and clarity is much more likely to follow when a child has been able to give vent to their feelings, freely and safely.

The more emotion that has been roused within a session, the longer the period required to reorientate to the demands of everyday situations. A check should be made that the child feels comfortable about returning to the next activity of their day. Additionally, it is useful to engage the child in talk about less emotive topics, e.g. school activities, pop music, etc., as a way of giving them back some sense of control.

The use of pictures offers a method of assisting the natural processes of healing. When people grieve, it assists them to tell their personal 'story', explore and express feelings, make sense of experience and helps them to modify or change their lives.

A COUNSELLING APPROACH TO HELP CHILDREN AND YOUNG PEOPLE COPE WITH LOSS

Not everyone who has contact with a grieving child will see themselves as a counsellor or feel natural confidence in working with complex and sensitive emotions. However, understanding some of the counselling

approaches can be helpful for parents/teachers/social work staff/relatives and will give an increased sense of confidence.

Counselling is a helping process which aims to assist the client, the child, in this instance, to understand their situation and feelings better, and with that insight to make appropriate responses and choices. What the counsellor offers are the conditions in which those insights and choices might flourish. The person-centred approach to counselling identifies three core conditions which must exist for the counselling to be effective; the counsellor must be:

> — **genuine**
> — **accepting**
> — **empathic.**

Children, more than any other client group, are likely to see if the person offering them help is not genuine. The lack of authenticity in the form of being patronising, or play-acting concern, will quickly result in the child being a reluctant participant in the helping venture. Acceptance, too, is of particular importance when counselling children, as they may have a confused awareness of the ways in which they are acceptable, particularly if adults have involved them in behaviour which they sense is wrong. Validating them as people and accepting their experience and perceptions non-judgmentally, permits a high level of trust; the basis for an open and productive relationship. Empathy is the quality which the counsellor needs to develop both to feel and appreciate the reality of the child's experience and to convey that insight sensitively to the child. Collectively these conditions are the basis for a highly sensitive relationship in which the needs of the child can be disclosed and choices explored.

The fundamental skill in all helping relationships is **listening.** It is something much more demanding than the distracted attention usually given by people in busy life situations. To listen effectively, the environment has to be conducive to the kind of sharing of painful material that counselling aims to encourage; ideally a warm, non-clinical, private room, free from interruptions. Listening in the helping context is being able to receive messages, both verbal and non-verbal, and to begin to process that information in order to understand, as clearly as possible, what the world of the client is like and how it is being experienced by them.

The child/young person's experience of loss may be totally unlike that of the carer or the way in which they interpret experiences. Listening and responding on the basis of how it is for the client is the first step, and needs to be the continuing guide, to the client's reality. Listening is at the heart of effective support and can be especially powerful with children, who often feel that adults do not listen to them.

The listening may not always come from a helping adult. Children and young people sharing with each other, may be the safest starting point for talking about loss. Clearly this may happen naturally, but for those engaged with groups of young people, e.g. teachers and youth leaders, it may be a source of support that can be actively encouraged.

Good listening liberates powerful emotions which may seem, in our culture of self-containment, overwhelming or inappropriate. Carers need to be clear that the expression of emotional pain, either through tears or anger, is part of the process of resolving pain and not just a definition of it. Memories of our own hurt feelings and a strong desire to 'make better' can stand in the way of accepting and staying alongside the distressed child.

It is important to remember, when faced with a very distressed child, that prohibiting emotional expression could sentence that child to a lonely and isolated process of dealing with their loss. The pain does not go away because it is invisible. Time spent, by carers, in understanding and working on the losses in their own life can be a prelude to more easy acceptance of the experience of others. This may be part of the supervision process which is described in the next section.

In all situations, whether of peer support or adult support, children need to be reassured about confidentiality, and given clear information about what may have to be shared with others, in their own interests, and what can remain totally confidential.

Helping a grieving child can be stressful. The raw emotions of a vulnerable young person can raise anxiety and a heavy sense of responsibility. Carers, therefore, must be clear about the child's needs and their own capacity to handle them. It is important to remember that children may be much less inhibited in their emotional expression, or conversely much less able to convey the depth of their feelings, than might be true for adults. Because of this, a wider range of responses may emerge. This range should not be forced into adult forms of expression, either by suppressing overt emotion or by persistently probing the withdrawn child. Rather, adult support should gently use whatever mode of expression is natural for the child.

Part of the process of obtaining the best help for a grieving child may be by referring on to someone else. Particular expertise may be required or else a different style of approach may be indicated (e.g. help from a man rather than a woman, someone who is more available, etc.). For all carers, in whatever capacity, it is essential that there is support to assist in the help that they are offering. Formal supervision will be an integral resource for professional counsellors. For others, having the listening support of someone able to offer understanding and insight into the loss situation being addressed, and awareness of the impact this may have at a personal level, is crucial. The best help for grieving children becomes available when there is appropriate and adequate support for their carers/counsellors. More information on supervision methods are included in the counselling books suggested in the bibliography.

The Process of Helping

There are a number of stages in the process. These include:

1.   Assessing the situation of loss for this particular child, by acquiring as much background information as is possible; circumstances of the loss, family situation, age and psychological resourcefulness of the child, etc. Gaining this information may be part of the initial contact with the child and when this is done sensitively, can be the means of creating a safe base from which the relationship can develop. At a later stage, feelings and behaviour need to be explored.

2.   Awareness about the need for help may come from outside the family (nursery staff, teachers, youth leaders, etc.). Be clear about who it is that perceives the need for help or support and how likely it is that such a view will be accepted within the family. Help may be sought by:

- **The child/young person.**
- **The parents.**
- **Another relative.**
- **Another carer, e.g. teacher, doctor.**
- **Others concerned, e.g. social worker, police.**

Help and support should always be negotiated directly with the child/young person, when it is someone else who has suggested a carer's involvement. However, the help offered to the child must recognise the views of the adult/parent who are most significant to their world, otherwise conflict and confusion are likely to result from different people offering different forms of help. Frequently, support for the adult/parent may be the best way of helping the child.

3.   Making initial contact with the child and continuous assessment of the situation must take account of the:

- **Level of distress.**
- **Context of the meeting with the child.**
- **Age (cognitive ability).**
- **What the child has been told about the loss.**

- What the child understands about what they have been told.
- What the child is feeling about the situation.
- What the child fears in the situation.
- What the child needs for their physical, emotional and social well-being.
- How the child perceives the carer's role, bearing in mind other ways in which the carer may already have a relationship with them.

4.   Communication is central to effective support. Issues which will affect communication are:
- The age of the child.
- The child's degree of comfort/discomfort in relating to adults.
- The child's degree of trust in adults.
- A high level of emotion may inhibit communication, i.e. the child is withdrawn.
- A high level of emotion may spill out uncontrollably.

Words may not be the easiest form of communication, especially with younger children, so their 'story' and the feelings which go with it may be better expressed through play, art (their own or other pictures), drama, story writing or reading, puppets, music, etc. As a carer/counsellor, it is an opportunity to be as creative as possible in finding an outlet which is comfortable and effective in exploring the nature and significance of loss.

5.   The aims of working with a child or young person who is coping with loss are to maximise their inner resourcefulness and the external support available; to assist in helping that young person know what their own emotional strengths are, and who are the people in their social world who can be relied upon for support. A counselling approach helps:
- To identify people and situations that offer security.
- The child to tell their 'story'.
- To confront the reality of what has been lost.
- To identify emotions and allow for their expression, e.g. tears, anger.
- To look at the practical consequences of the loss and decide what other changes need to be made as a result, e.g. the demands of living with step-parents.
- To provide opportunities for the child to make sense of their experience, i.e. how it fits with their view of the world.
- To assist in looking at the opportunities for the future.

6.   Ending the work with a child or young person who has been coping with a significant loss, needs to be done very carefully. It can be the model for handling loss and change well, or it can be another example of a child feeling let down and exposed to the vulnerability of external events. Always try to:
- Plan for the ending of the support work.
- Involve the child in the planning.
- Review what has been achieved.
- Clarify the sources of support that will be available for the child now that this help is ending.
- Give space for an appropriate 'goodbye'.

Conclusion

Counselling is a way of using a human relationship, in its most sensitive form, to facilitate the help of another. This sensitivity allows for the most painful disclosure of events and feelings, a process of release and reappraisal. At its best, not only may it allow for the resolution of a past hurt but it can also provide a model for sound relationship-making in the future. Children who are struggling to come to terms with loss and tragedy especially need support of this kind.

Part 2

SITUATIONS OF LOSS IN CHILDHOOD

Introduction

In Part 2, the range, the context and the nature of loss faced by children and young people is explored. The external and internal mechanisms which facilitate or impede a natural resolution of grief are examined. These issues are important areas of understanding for all those who work with grieving children.

Where the material is used for training purposes, each section should be photocopied and used as the basis for discussion. For practitioners working with children in loss situations it provides background reading and reference material.

Childhood is characterised by change. Some changes are imperceptible, while others are dramatic and seen as milestones in physical, intellectual or social development. The passage from conception to maturity brings a constant shifting of physical and social reality, and adaptations to that reality have to be made. Signs of growing maturity come as children demonstrate that experience in one situation has equipped them with skills for another. The development of resources in all areas of human capacity — physical dexterity, intellectual competence, social effectiveness — occurs most easily where the process is positive and nurturing.

Change which permits some element of choice will help lessen the sense of loss at times of transition. Choice increases the sense of control and reduces the sense of 'being at the mercy' of external events. Where change proves to be traumatic and emotionally overwhelming for the child, two things will happen; first, emotional resources will feel less than adequate for the adjustments which have to be made, and second, the process of acquiring new social skills will be disrupted or even damaged. In these circumstances adult support and intervention are indicated.

There are four dimensions in which loss and change can be experienced:

1. Lost and damaging relationships

Relationships are central to a human sense of well-being and for a child they are crucial both for short-term and long-term emotional health. The death of a parent will clearly be psychologically and socially traumatic. Equally, the break-up of parental marriage and the social disruption and reorientation which will follow, will produce a level of emotional trauma comparable to a bereavement. Such changed social circumstances will be readily obvious to people in contact with the child, but the events which precede them may not be so easily recognised; for instance, marital disharmony and terminal illness which herald loss and call for adjustments, may be invisible to the outsider.

The breaking of relationship bonds is not the only circumstance in which the child will have to experience change and loss. Relationships which are damaging or confusing will, at worst, set the pattern for unhealthy future relationships, and, at least, undermine healthy interpersonal development. Abused children, in addition to the psychological and/or physical trauma they experience, will have lost the opportunity to develop trust and caring; qualities lost in the sense that they have not been received, but also lost because they will not know how to give them.

Relationship difficulties play a significant part in what has to be addressed when working with children, especially as support and recovery from loss is also very dependent upon establishing good quality therapeutic relationships. Where the child's natural social support system includes negative adult relationships — absent or damaged — developing therapeutic contact can be difficult, raising feelings of ambivalence and mistrust in the child. Particular care is essential in building trust and ensuring clarity of purpose in the relationship.

2. Physical and intellectual development

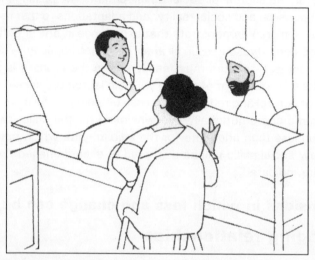

is of central concern to parents; the satisfactory progress of the infant is measured in recognisable goals of achievement, monitored by health visitors and school nurses. Where the child begins life with health problems, the anxieties which accompany illness and disability become part of their early inheritance. Some of the disabling symptoms may only have an impact on carers/parents at the stage where the child would ordinarily be achieving a measure of independence. At that stage, the grief of the parents related to the disappointments of having a child that is not healthy, will begin to emerge. The child him/herself will be exposed to those parental emotions. They frequently capture those disappointments and resentments, and begin to feel a loss of wholeness.

Illness and disability occurring during the course of childhood may affect growth and development, or indeed lead to death. As with congenital disorders or birth injury, the onset of illness, even non-life threatening and transitory illness, will be the cause for parental concern. The adult responses in such circumstances will contribute to the child's own self image and sense of security. Their sense of what has been lost will be an echo of the messages, overt and covert, which have been given by adults, and will be characterised by a tendency to lack physical independence and freedom to choose activities and life directions.

Issues concerned with medical treatment, pain, limited potential to enter fully into life opportunities and even the prospect of death, may be the focus for carers working with this dimension of loss in childhood.

3. Economic disadvantage is the reality of social experience for many children. Low family income arising from unemployment, low pay, and lone parent situations set the scene for a spiral of deprivation. Poor housing and inadequate diet are likely to follow and contribute to poor health, limited opportunity for stimulation of physical, intellectual and social growth, in a situation where other accompanying features of poverty may include crime, substance abuse, etc.

The political context is part of the economic reality of social, educational and health provisions. Rather than countering disadvantage, it may reinforce it. The level of social provision and the ethos in which it is

14

provided, has in recent times led to a broadening of the gap between those who fare well in society, and those who do not. The result is that there is likely to be a large number of people from disadvantaged groups requiring help in all areas of welfare provision; needs become cumulative as resources diminish. The

consequence of this disadvantage is limited emotional and social resourcefulness, resulting in low self-esteem.

Children may not always come to the attention of professional carers solely on account of the economic disadvantage of their family. Nevertheless, the impact of 'loss' caused by economic factors should be addressed by those who are in contact with young people, e.g. teachers, as they cope with lifestyles and circumstances that marginalise them in the society in which they live. Such marginalisation is a key feature for individuals and communities where whole groups of people are subject to disadvantage on the basis of poverty, class, race and gender. The wider social and political implications fall outside the immediate focus of this material, but the reality of individual economic disadvantage is an important feature to recognise when focusing on loss in childhood.

4. Unfulfilled ambitions

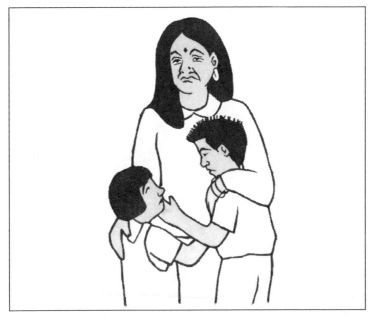

Childhood and its transitory, if lengthy, nature is programmed much more by forces external to the child than by the child's own aspirations. Nevertheless, much of childhood activity, whether in school or in play, is a rehearsal for future life situations. This being so the child will begin to invest mental and emotional energy into those things which are perceived by them as purposeful or pleasing. Goals will be set by the child, by parents and by teachers. Sometimes they are realistic, at other times they are unrealistic, or merely represent the desire of the parent to have their own needs met through their children. Where this is the situation the scene is set for disappointment. How disappointment is handled will determine not only the outcome of a current failure but will contribute to future responses where ambitions remain unfulfilled. The timid or the cynical child may have been thwarted in a way which makes them unwilling to take risks in the future and ungenerous in the face of other peoples' success.

This category of loss may exist alone or accompany any of the categories previously described. Always try to consider all of a child's circumstances, including:

- Broken and/or damaging relationships which may rob a child of what they want for themselves. For example, parental separation may result in confused and complex relationships when the child would choose the simplicity and tranquility of both parents loving each other and living in the same home.

- Illness or disability, whether of the child or some other significant person in their life may constrain them emotionally and socially and deprive them of a lifestyle which they would like. Brothers and sisters of a dying child may have to conceal their own needs so much, that when the death does occur, there may be a severe emotional and/or behavioural backlash against parents and friends and the child who has died.

- Economic disadvantage in modern western society, when set amongst images and observable realities of affluence, will contribute to a sense of loss which may be characterised by depression; a depression which is the result not only of loss but also of hopelessness. Where such conditions persist, the child may be severely psychologically debilitated, or begin to protest and give expression to frustration in anti-social ways.

- Unfulfilled ambitions which are often manifest in depression and/or poor self esteem.

THE CONTEXT OF LOSS

1. Home

Forming relationships and the context of experience begins and continues in the home. Both short term and long term well-being are determined by the quality of the care given, and the emotional and social stability which is engendered by this. Where loss and change are experienced within the supportive and nurturing context of the family, the natural capacity for surviving healthily will be at its maximum; emotional and social resources will be available to meet the needs of changed circumstances, even when these are profound losses through death, illness or economic misfortune. Nevertheless, the normal healthy functioning of the family

16

group may sometimes need the reinforcing support of outside carers.

For other children, home may be the context of loss, because home never offers the security which is necessary for healthy development, and therefore the child has lost out in the process of discovering their own human potential. This may be the case when carers are inadequate, or abuse their caring role.

2. School

School is a central social experience for all children and contributes to the cumulative store of good or bad experiences in the child's life. For some, the whole process of attending school is problematic while for others it may only be passing incidents which are difficult to handle. The tendency for children to be categorised rather than individualised, is part of the reality of social community life. Characteristic of the categorisation of children is labelling where they become identified as lazy, intelligent, disruptive, high-flier, amusing, no good, etc. This may help to reinforce behaviour which is deemed appropriate within society, but it may produce psychological pressure which is temporarily or permanently damaging to the healthy functioning of the child, especially if the label sticks and the child cannot break out of the perception others have of them.

Pressures of other kinds apply with the competitive element of educational performance. For some children this may be the spur to achievement, while for others it might create a long term sense of inferiority. The way in which school life will contribute, or not, to the healthy psychosocial development of a child will depend on how family life reinforces it or contradicts it. Where messages in both 'social worlds' are consistent, the child is more likely to function in an unambiguous way, but where there is a discrepancy, the child may be unclear as to their social role.

School is a central social environment, which may produce its own problems of loss through the undermining of the child's developing sense of self. It is also the context of much change. Transition is at the heart of the journey through education. Where the resourcefulness of the child is equal to the demands of those changes, then engagement with new situations will happen naturally. Where the school environment itself and/or family difficulties arise at the time of a significant transition, teachers and parents will be confronted with the emotional and behavioural consequences of a child in crisis. Adults projecting a false gloss of ''it's something we all have to go through'' or ''in a few weeks you will have forgotten all about the difficulties you are facing now'' may serve only to maximise the emotional trauma, and create precedents for not dealing with painful events in an open and healthy way.

School is also the context in which disturbances at home will come to light. This may not always occur in an obvious way, which makes responding more complex. Signs of tiredness, general malaise, irritability, reduced performance, changed patterns of relating to peers, behaviour problems, may emerge either as single or multiple symptoms. These complex symptoms can pose problems for teachers, especially when possible abuse is suspected. Uncertainty about appropriate intervention can lead to a passive approach, rationalised by feeling that if problems are ignored they will go away. Where co-operation between home and school can be facilitated then the child is likely to have the best possible support in what they are experiencing as a difficult situation. In circumstances of bereavement, marital breakdown, etc., the teacher may be in the best position to offer stable adult support in a world of shifting realities.

3. Informal Social Groups (youth groups, interest groups, peer groups).

Within these groups, the child has more potential freedom to relate and choose activities that reflect their own preferences. There may, however, still be echoes of parental/adult wishes within these groupings, e.g. younger children may pursue interests such as sport or music because that is what schools or parents desire for them. Where these groups are more freely chosen, the possibilities for self-expression, development and support can be considerable.

Adult leaders in such groups can be very significant in offering support to a child who is coping with a loss. Such help may come from an awareness of the stresses which the child is facing, and continuing the routines of the group with low-key attention to the child, or by being more overtly available to listen to what the child wishes/needs to disclose. Children often use such adults as advisors and role models. The power that is invested in such relationships needs to be understood and used appropriately by those adults who care for, or lead the young people's groups.

Peer groups can be more problematic in that they may either contribute to the sense of worth felt by a child, or may reinforce their alienation. Such groups may also be units of collective protest against authority. In such situations, a child may develop a keener sense of 'self' at a personal level, but be more out of step with their own social world.

Loss of a significant friend through death, moving house, or a break in a relationship should be recognised as an important stimulus to grief in a child or young person. Even short-lived friendships can be very intense and important. The forming of friendships is a significant development in the life of a child and the freedom of choice is important to individual self-esteem. This being so, it should be recognised that there is a direct connection between the intensity of engagement in a relationship and the intensity of feeling associated with a break in such a relationship.

CHILDHOOD ATTACHMENT

Reference has been made throughout the text to loss as an experience of transition and as an experience of more traumatic breaks in life stability. John Bowlby and others have explored the connections between attachment and loss and have suggested patterns of reaction to separation, which have added to an understanding of this experience. Three phases have been identified, when a child is separated from their mother-figure. The first stage occurs immediately after the separation and is characterised by protest, the second stage is despair where the energy of the earlier stage is replaced by apathy, and the third stage (where the separation persists) is one of detachment.

The establishment of the very early bond, which develops between the new born child and the mother

figure, is seen as setting the pattern for psychological stability in the child. Where the bond is reinforced by consistent attention to the physical needs of the child then emotional stability will follow. Where the attention is inconsistent, or there are significant periods of absence, then the child will begin to show symptoms, even from a very early age, of the searching and restlessness which are part of the grieving process.

Short term breaks in contact can be incorporated into experience positively if the care is resumed and again offered consistently. In such a situation the child will develop a tolerance of separation from their carer with no psychological ill effect. Where there is inconsistent care and lengthy separation, heightened anxiety will impede the healthy development of the child. The pattern of instability will lead to insecurity and varied emotional and behavioural reactions, such as personality disturbance, anxiety, anger, depression and emotional detachment. Reversing such a trend will require the establishment of, or the return to, the provision of care.

Engaging with a child at the point of their need; when ill or fearful, by showing affection, involvement in the child's activities and encouraging inclusive behaviour (e.g. involving the child in family rituals, etc.) are ways of encouraging attachment. Carers need to be able to reinforce attachment in a number of these areas, particularly at a time of loss or change. This will enable even the child who has previously been denied the opportunity to develop positive attachments, a supported experience from which to build healthy relationships.

GRIEF — THE RESPONSE TO LOSS

Grief is a complex psychological and social response to loss. It is produced by significant change or trauma, in which a person experiences a profound disturbance in the emotional or social realities of their world.

Grief is often simply seen as an emotion, but other dimensions of human experience are stimulated by loss and change. There is:

☐ A physical response
☐ A psychological response
☐ A social response
☐ An intellectual response
☐ A spiritual response.

It is important to recognise all of these aspects when looking at the human experience of loss.

The intensity of grief and its persistence is hugely variable but it has a number of characteristics which can be identified, even within those variations. (Refer to Murray Parkes, Kubler-Ross, Worden in the bibliography.)

1. Denial

Denial is an immediate rejection of the reality of bad news. What cannot be assimilated is rejected. Where there has been some preparation, e.g. a terminal illnes, discussion prior to the breakdown of a relationship, etc., the denial will be less intense and shorter lived. Where there has been no opportunity to consider the loss in prospect, then the denial is likely to be a very important part of the early grieving response. Psychologically it enables the emotions to be protected from what would be overwhelming. There is an anaesthetic quality to denial which holds the pain at bay until enough psychological srength has been marshalled to respond to it. In the early stages a statement such as ''I can't believe this has happened'' is common, but later a more persistent denial can occur where the person behaves as if nothing has changed in their world. The clues to this longer term suppression of reality may occur where symptoms of distress such as nightmares, bed wetting, etc., indicate that the loss has not been accommodated in spite of the more overt message that 'all is well'.

For children, the natural mechanisms of denial are compounded by the tendency of adults to exclude them from situations that are deemed too painful for them to handle. It is important, therefore, for carers not to confuse a lack of information with denial or shock; what is not known cannot be denied. Care must be taken in giving information; it should be clear and unambiguous. Grandad's death is not accurately explained by ''grandad has gone away''. The child who remembers grandad going on holiday last year, will see no need for an emotional response.

Everyday explanations for very particular events may leave the child confused and responding apparently inappropriately. For example, at the beginning they may make no response to grandad's absence, but later on they may show a concern about any 'going away' because sometimes going away means not coming back. These confusions are particularly significant in the life of the abused child, where relationships are conducted on a different basis in private and in public. Here the child will probably be given an overt message to deny the experience of abuse, alongside the covert message that this is acceptable behaviour. A sense of numbness and shock, with its characteristic distancing from reality, should not be taken as evidence that the child has accepted or come to terms with the loss(es).

2. Emotional Anguish

When the psychological purpose of denial, which is to protect, begins to subside, **the anguish of the loss** emerges powerfully. Children have not yet acquired adult inhibitions in this direction, and may be particularly expressive of the emotional pain they are feeling. Feeling powerless engenders protest, and the emotion of protest is anger; anger may be directed towards:

— **The source of pain (death, divorce).**
— **The person or object lost.**
— **Other everyday situations that feel difficult to cope with (exams, house move).**
— **Others unconnected with the loss but who are in an inferior power relationship, e.g. a younger child.**

Anger should be seen as natural, but support should be given to ensure that its expression is not counter productive.

Guilt too is characteristic of grief. At certain stages in a child's development, psychological growth is marked by a new sense of powerfulness which is not consistent with reality. For example, the three-year-old who suddenly learns how to manipulate people and situations may have a very mistaken view of their part in a death or parental dispute, seeing their behaviour as having contributed to the disastrous outcome. Such misunderstandings can be difficult to resolve for the young child whose cognative insights are limited. For the teenager who similarly experiences the powerfulness of being an emergent adult, counselling around loss is very important. Distinguishing fact and fantasy, and recognising the difference between wishing that father was dead and causing his death are very different.

Guilt may also arise where children feel that they have failed to comply with parental wishes. For example, "Mum would not have become ill if I had helped with the housework". Such unhelpful and even damaging connections are made when grieving adults project their own anger on to their children, e.g. "Daddy might not have left if you hadn't been a naughty boy". This culture of blame is swiftly internalised by the child and incorporated into a response to loss. Sometimes the child who protests most vigorously is covering a deep seated sense of their personal responsibility for a loss. This period of anguish may become further confused if current life situations, not connected with the loss, are difficult, e.g. examination pressures, peer group tensions, etc. Disentangling the painful elements may be as problematic for the young person as it is for parents or teachers.

Other forceful grief reactions, which can be psychologically and socially disruptive include:

- **Anxiety.**
- **Dismay.**
- **Longing.**

- **Shame.**
- **Vivid and/or obsessive memories.**

3. Partial adjustment

Resolving grief alongside the often painful process of growing up, can seem to keep the anguish 'centre stage'

for a long time. The phase of **partial accommodation** of the loss may, therefore, be a very fluctuating one in which the child will seem to be making some adjustments one day only to return to a period of protest the next. Whether coming to terms with the loss is transitory or permanent, it will still be characterised by certain features. These will include a more introverted emotional response such as brooding or depression, often associated with physical apathy and reduced energy.

Reflection on how the child would "like things to be", may be voiced or merely be part of their silent and perhaps sullen, musing. This element of emotional introversion is balanced by a greater capacity to engage at a social level with changed circumstances. For example, there may be evidence of settling into a new home environment or forming more positive bonds with step-relatives, etc. It is a period of recognising that the personal world has changed, and responding to those changes with more social energy but with a measure of emotional uncertainty. At this stage, the child or young person may seem harder to reach as they seek to resolve internal emotional tensions and external social pressures.

4. Acceptance

Resolving grief comes when an acceptance of the loss is incorporated into the present life situation; the scars of pain will remain but they no longer dominate all life experience. The evidence for this stage having been reached, by adults, is their capacity to form new relationships, re-negotiate old ones, and look positively towards the future. With children, their need to comply with adult 'scripts' may lead us to believe they have reached this point before they actually have; their dependent status has given them neither the choice nor the capacity to respond without reference to the adult world. This being so, if they are under pressure to accommodate new social circumstances, they may appear to do so without betraying the reality of their own discomfort in the face of change. Carers should be alert to this, and distinguish between a child's obedient conformity, and their capacity to freely choose aspects of living — relationships, life-style, etc., which are appropriate for them.

Conclusion

While these responses to grief have been described sequentially, it is important to remember that there is neither a helpful timescale which can be applied to them, nor do the elements of grief follow a predetermined pattern. The triggering of painful memories by events like birthdays and anniversaries can continue long after social adjustments seem to have been made. Such fluctuation in grief and its expression must be recognised, especially in children. If the grief is not satisfactorily resolved, new loss and change will reactivate old grief, thus multiplying pain. Such a cumulative process is likely to be damaging to the long term psychological and social well-being of the child or young person. Loss resolved will give a positive experience to enable future losses to be handled with more confidence. Unresolved loss demands that old and new wounds have to be handled together — an overwhelming task for a child.

HOW ADULTS UNDERSTAND GRIEF AND THE IMPLICATIONS FOR GRIEVING CHILDREN AND YOUNG PEOPLE

Children learn either by following an observable model or by being directed to respond to situations in a given way. This is as true in situations of loss as it is in any other learning context. Four possible patterns of grief result from the way in which adults interact with children in situations of loss.

1. **Where parents/adults are open and unambiguous** in their grieving, children will have a clear model to follow

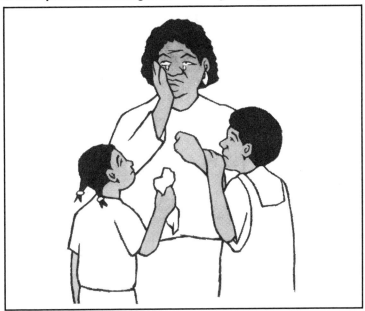

and are likely to express their grief with every confidence about its appropriateness. In this situation, parents/adults are likely to offer or make available the kind of appropriate support which will sustain the child.

For carers outside the family — teachers, counsellors, etc., intervention can straightforwardly complement family support.

2. **Where families operate with very clearly defined, individual roles,** behavioural scripts may prescribe the

ways in which family members can operate. For example, in situations of crisis, dad can be angry, mum sad, the children are indulged, etc. Feelings and experiences which take individual family members outside the certainty of their own script, may result in some aspects of grief being expressed, and others remaining dormant or vicariously expressed by someone else in the family. Support, in such a situation, will demand a raising of awareness of the limitation of scripts and encouragement for each member to explore and express the full range of experience and feeling related to loss.

3. **Some adults deny the existence of grief in children.** It may be rationalised — ''they get over things

quickly'', ''children adapt easily'', ''children soon forget'', ''they seem okay''. In such a context children quickly pick up the message that they need to function as if nothing had disturbed their world. While it may be possible to suppress some responses, grief may spill out in the form of physical symptoms, illness or behavioural disturbance. (The latter being veiled manifestations of the emotional and social disruption which the child is having to handle.)

Some adults may not overtly deny the reality of grief in children, but find the expression of pain so difficult to cope with that they feel compelled to comfort and 'make better', thus constraining the child to suppress their grief.

In such families, the pain may only be visible in the adult(s). Here the carer may have to assist the development of parental insight and/or offer that support to the child which is unavailable in the family context.

4. **Adults who control or suppress their own grief** may also seek to control and suppress their children's grief.

''Big boys don't cry'' being a typical model of not permitting children and young people to grieve. In such circumstances, when the child's pain begins to show, the adult may either welcome the vicarious expression of their own hurt through the child, or swiftly seek a form of help which will enable the child to "get over it quickly".

In such families, the pain may only be visible in the children. The carer's role will be to both facilitate parental insight, and to offer support to the child.

Conclusion

The varied situations requiring the recognition of, and response to, children's grief, needs to be understood by teachers and carers, who may only be given information about the child's reaction on the basis of the faulty awareness of the adult/parent. Sometimes, the grieving parent needs support in recognising the child's pain. In other scenarios, the evident pain of the child needs to be seen as normal and also that it is perfectly correct for parents to be showing grief too. Parent reactions, whether they are overt or suppressed, provide the significant climate in which a child has to experience their grief; in some instances the reaction of a remaining parent, whether following a death or a divorce, will have more impact on a child than loss of the other parent. Where parents are in tune with their own and their children's grief, outside carers may be required to lend support to an existing healthy process of working through the grief.

SYMPTOMS OF GRIEF IN CHILDREN AND YOUNG PEOPLE

Grief affects people physically, emotionally, socially, intellectually and spiritually. The most obvious symptoms of distress are likely to show themselves in some form of emotional expression and in some measure of disturbance in behaviour. However, as we have seen in the earlier section which looks at functioning in the family, scripted or limiting messages given to children when they face loss, will reduce their capacity to make appropriate and spontaneous responses to new experience. It is important, therefore, to be clear about some of the symptoms which may not appear to be related to loss as well as describing the more obvious symptoms of grief.

Under 5s

From a very early age, children will begin to respond to the absence of the significant people in their world. Such absences are experienced and not understood; the response is to the experience and not to an intellectual reflection upon it. A child will not understand the reasons for, or the significance of death or parental desertion, but their experience of a changed world will be very real. For the child old enough to make a verbal response to their circumstances, limited understanding and insight will be demonstrated in what they say. For example: "When will X (dead baby sister) be coming back?" Curiosity about factual aspects of death and loss, which may seem insensitive to the adult, are characteristic of the young child's engagement with new experiences.

Physical manifestations of the disturbance caused by a loss may include — frequent colds, rashes, constipation, wetting and soiling. Behaviourally, the child may be subject to tantrums, excessive crying and changes in sleep patterns.

5-8 years

At this stage of development children begin to understand more about cause and effect and the qualities of experience. For instance, the idea about the "foreverness" of death is beginning to be grasped. The increased awareness about the nature of experience also permits a greater sense of empathy with others; realisation that loss and change affect other people is combined with an increased ability to respond to them. Nevertheless, aspects of this awareness are still based on misconceptions and there is a measure of fantasy about the loss experience. A child's anxieties, therefore, may be based on their own imaginings and fantasies, rather than upon objective reality. For this reason, carers need to listen and be sensitive to those elements of feeling which children need to express and understand. At this stage some pressure may exist for feelings to be suppressed and the school context may be one in which children feel the need to look "okay" to their peers.

As at an earlier stage, proneness to colds and viral infections may typify the physical responses to loss. There may also be the onset of conditions such as asthma and eczema. Night wetting and soiling can arise and the symptoms themselves give rise to anxiety in the child and parent. Disturbed sleeping may be manifest in sleep walking or nightmares. School refusing may accompany an anxiety about the safety of the remaining parent, where the other has died or deserted. The child may become withdrawn and have some fear about their own security.

8-12 years

Abstract thinking develops at this stage and the possibility of one's own death becomes a more focused thought, especially where the child is bereaved. Other kinds of loss — separation of parents, disability, etc., will also be understood and the consequences for the child incorporated into their thinking. As the importance of coping behaviour is reinforced by adults, the child may have fewer opportunities to explore and express underlying feelings.

The emergence of sexuality with complexities of feeling about self, and relatedness to others, may be especially poignant for children who have been the subject of abuse or who are having to resolve feelings about parents following the breakup of a marriage.

Physically there may be an exacerbation of pre-existing conditions such as asthma, diabetes, etc., and the possible development of acting-out strong feelings, for example fighting at school, etc.

Adolescence

Adolescence is itself a period of loss and change; physical, emotional and social emergence into adulthood brings its own anxieties and apprehensions. Where this life transition is combined with other experiences of separation or loss the reactions are likely to be complex. If the person who dies or deserts is significant as a source of identification, particular attention will need to be paid to the process of mourning and disengagement. The adolescent will grieve in largely similar ways to adults, but may be much more overtly moody and/or depressed. Knowing how to show sadness and gain comfort without seeming to regress to being a child can be a dilemma for a young person; it may be handled by denying needs and feelings and thus aspects of the grief remain unresolved.

In a body which is changing there may be anxiety about health and altered physical appearance. Such anxiety may show itself in a measure of hypochondria or changed eating patterns such as obsessive slimming. The grief reactions of guilt and anger may be exaggerated and acted out in anti-social behaviour such as substance abuse, shop lifting and inappropriate relationships.

Conclusion

Age related symptoms are important to recognise, but they must be seen as having variable application; some children will have acquired an intellectual awareness about death, for example, at an earlier stage than others. The position in the family may determine areas of knowledge and social skill which put some children ahead of other members of their peer group in some of these areas. Nevertherless enabling symptoms of grief to emerge in any or all dimensions of knowledge, feeling and behavioural expression, is crucial to making an appropriate response.

BIBLIOGRAPHY

Axline, V., 1971. Dibs: In search of self, Penguin.

Ayalon, Ofra, 1987. Rescue, Nord.

Bowlby, John, 1981. Attachment and Loss: Vol 3 Loss, Penguin.

Brown, Elaine, 1979. The Surprise Present, Lion.

Capacchione, Lucia, 1989. The Creative Journal for Children, Shambbala.

Carle, Eric, 1974. The Very Hungry Caterpillar, Puffin.

Crompton, Margaret, 1990. Attending to Children, Edward Arnold.

Crompton, Margaret, 1992. Children and Counselling, Edward Arnold.

Dryden, W. (Ed.), 1991. Individual Therapy, O.U.P.

Dyregrov, Atle, 1991. Grief in Children: a handbook for adults, Jessica Kingsley.

Erikson, E., 1965. Eight Ages of Man — Childhood and Society, Penguin.

Gatliffe, Eleanor D., 1988. Death in the Classroom, Epworth.

Gersie, Alida, 1992. Storymaking in Bereavement, Jessica Kingsley.

Grollman, Earl A. (Ed.), 1967. Explaining Death to Children, Beacon Press, Boston.

Grollman, Earl A., 1976. Talking about Death, Beacon Press, Boston.

Hardy, M., Heyes, S., Crews, J., Rookes, P., Wren, K., 1990. Studying Child Psychology, Weidenfeld and Nicolson.

Jewett, C., 1984. Helping Children Cope with Separation and Loss, Batsford.

Kennedy, Eugene, 1981. Crisis Counselling, Gill & Macmillan.

Krementz, Jill, 1983. How it Feels when a Parent Dies, Gollanz.

Kubler-Ross, Elisabeth, 1978. On Death and Dying, Tavistock.

Lendrum, Susan, Syme, Gabrielle, 1992. Gift of Tears, Tavistock/Routledge.

Machin, Linda, Holt, Carole, 1988. All Change, C.E.M.

Machin, Linda, 1990. Looking at Loss, Longman.

Macklin, Jim, 1991, Remembering and Going On, Le Pine, Australia.

Murgatroyd, S., 1985. Counselling and Helping, Methuen.

Murray Parkes, Colin, 1972. Bereavement, Pelican.

Nelson-Jones, Richard, 1990. Human Relationship Skills, Cassell.

Noonan, Ellen, 1983. Counselling Young People, Methuen.

Raphael, Beverley, 1984. The Anatomy of Bereavement, Unwin Hyman.

Rudolph, Marguerita, 1978. Should the Children Know?, Schocken, N.Y.

Selby, Jan, 1975. The Day Grandma Died, C.I.O., London.

Smith, Doris B., 1975. A Taste of Blackberries, Heinemann.

St Christopher's Hospice, 1989. Someone Special has Died.

Tompkins, Susan (Ed.), 1979. Is Death the End?, C.E.M.

Varley, Susan, 1992. Badger's Parting Gift, Picture Lions.

Viorst, Judith, 1971. The Tenth Good Thing About Barney, Collins.

Wells, Rosemary, 1988. Helping the Children Cope with Grief, Sheldon.

Williams, Guinevere, Ross, Julia, 1983. When People Die, Macdonald.

Wolff, Sula, 1981. Children Under Stress, Penguin.

Worden, J. William, 1991. Grief Counselling and Grief Therapy, Tavistock/Routledge.

Wynnejones, Pat, 1985. Children, Death and Bereavement, S.U.

Zolotow, Charlotte, 1978. My Grandson Lew, Windmill.

Part 3

PICTURE RESOURCES

This part of the manual is divided into four sections. The pictures and worksheets are the 'core' of the material, which can be directly used with children and young people who need assistance to work through 'grief' and 'loss situations'.

Full instructions and guidelines for using the pictures, story lines and worksheets are contained at the beginning of Part 1 of the manual. We recommend that before using the material contained in this part of the manual, that you become conversant with the rest of the information contained in Parts 1 and 2, which deal specifically with counselling and therapeutic methods and the context of, and responses to loss.

The range of visual materials contained in Part 3 includes:

(A)   STORY LINES

(B)   PICTURE SITUATIONS

(C)   TRIGGER PICTURES

(D)   WORK SHEETS

PICTURE STORY LINES — A1

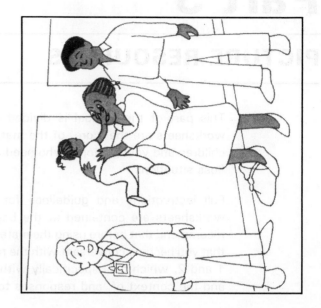

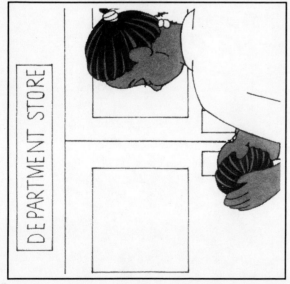

PICTURE STORY LINES — A2

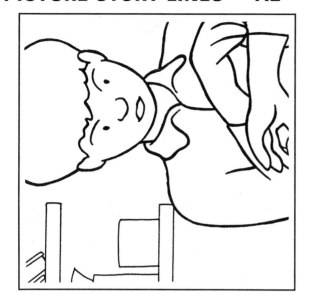 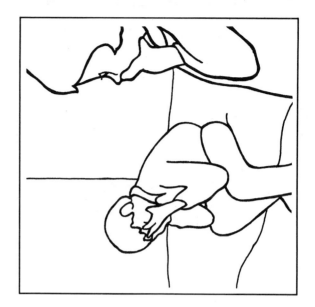

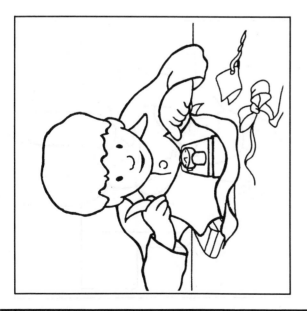 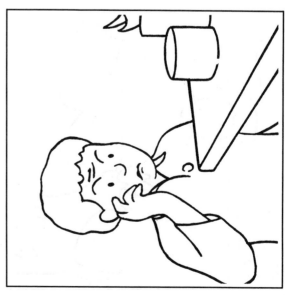

PICTURE STORY LINES — A3

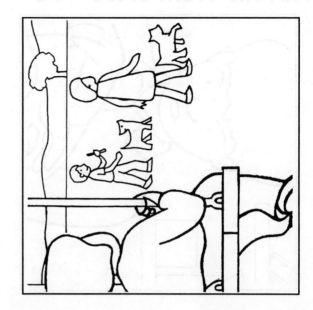

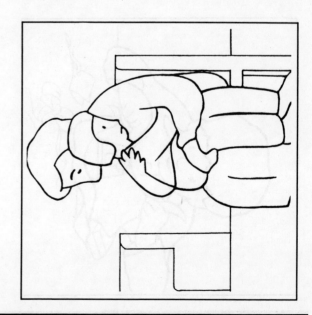

PICTURE STORY LINES — A4

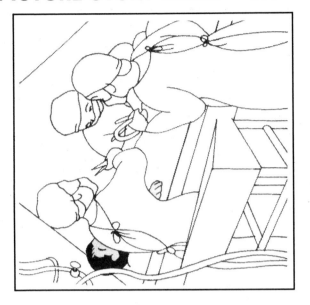 

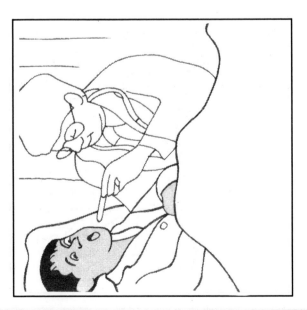 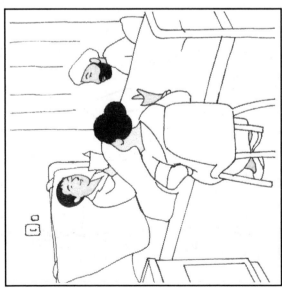

PICTURE STORY LINES — A5

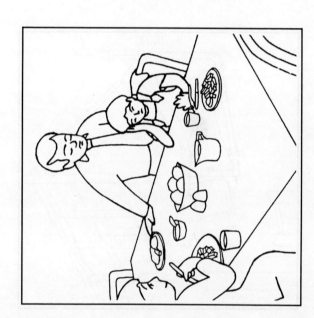

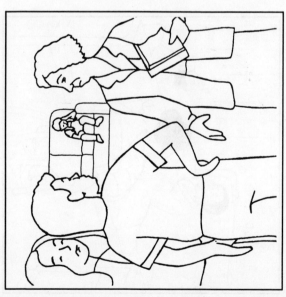

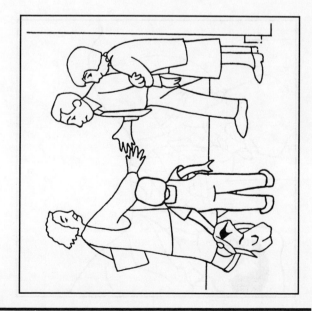

PICTURE SITUATIONS — B6

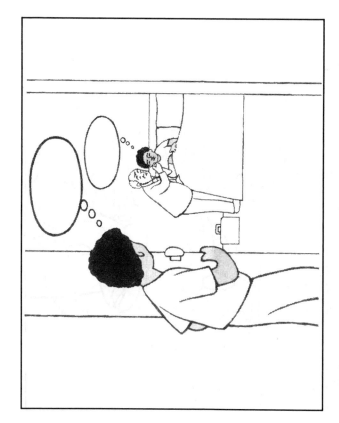

PICTURE SITUATIONS — B7

PICTURE SITUATIONS — B8

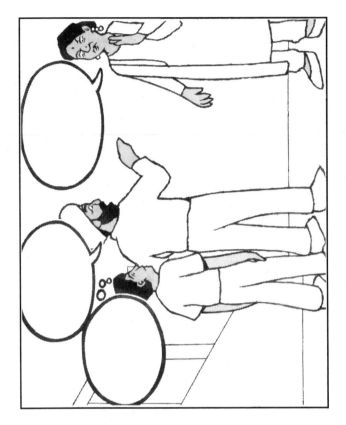
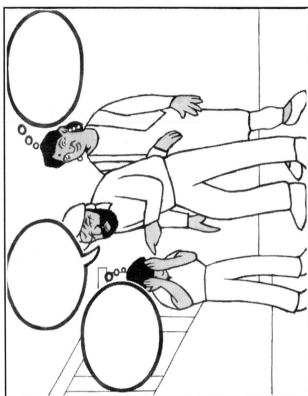

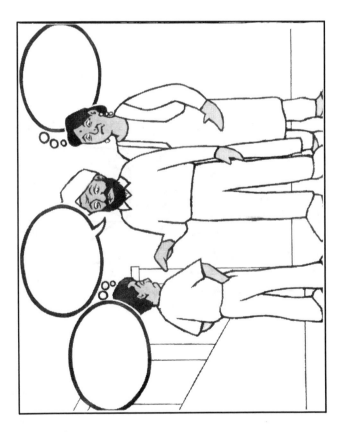

PICTURE SITUATIONS — B9

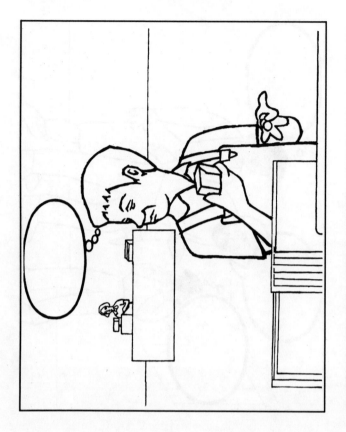
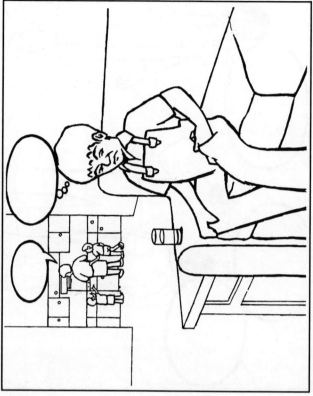
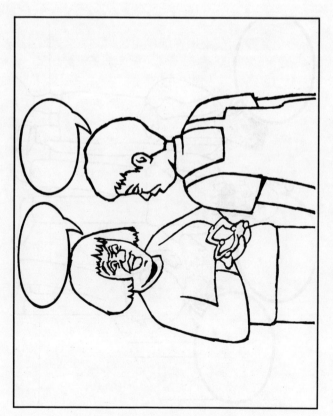
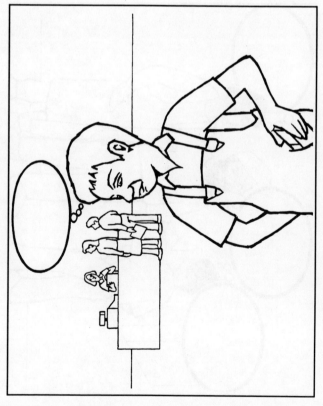

INDIVIDUAL TRIGGER PICTURES — C10

INDIVIDUAL TRIGGER PICTURES — C11

© Longman

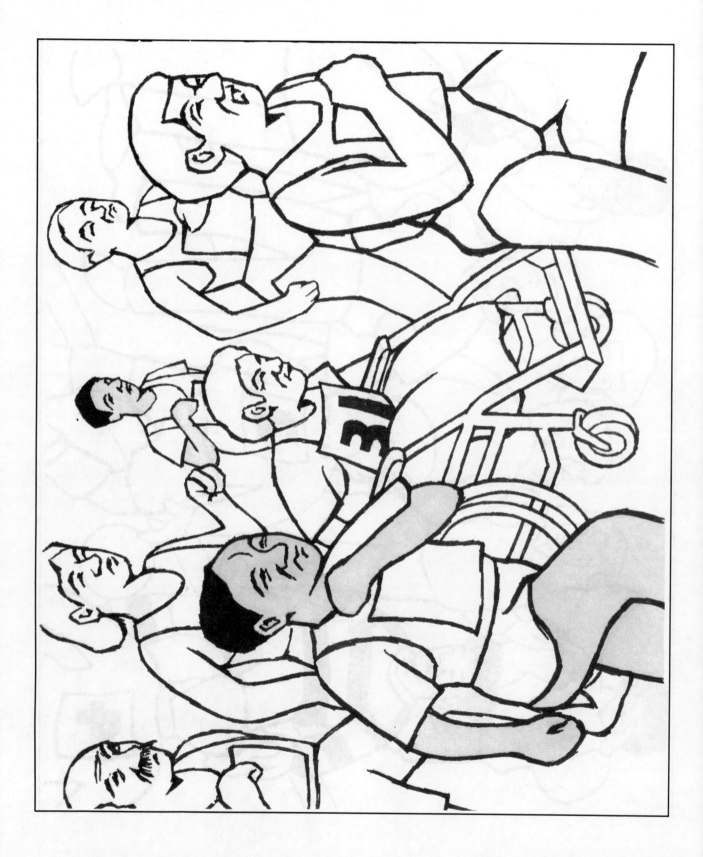

INDIVIDUAL TRIGGER PICTURES — C12

INDIVIDUAL TRIGGER PICTURES — C13

INDIVIDUAL TRIGGER PICTURES — C14

43

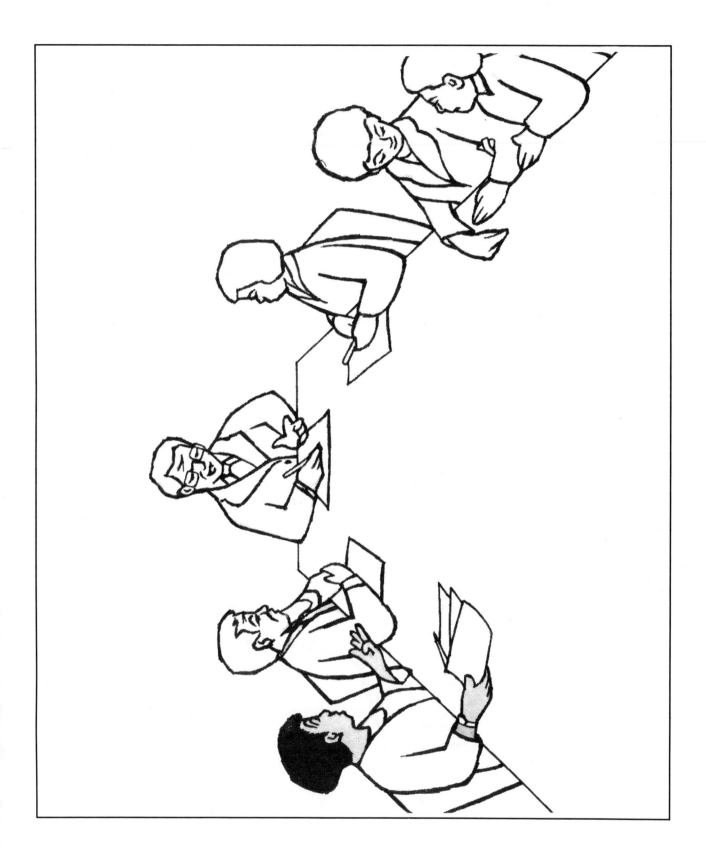

INDIVIDUAL TRIGGER PICTURES — C15

INDIVIDUAL TRIGGER PICTURES — C16

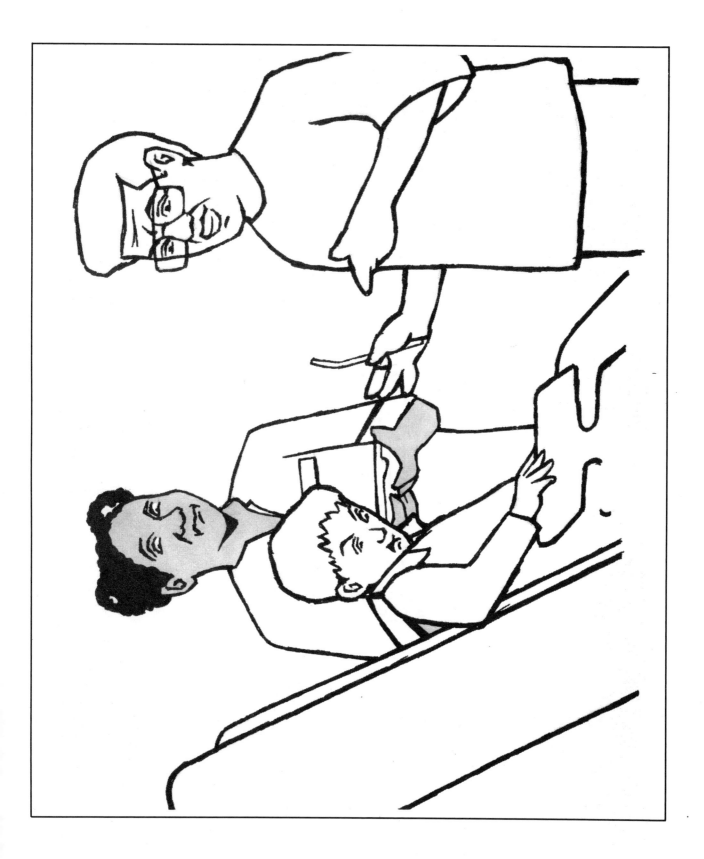

INDIVIDUAL TRIGGER PICTURES — C17

© Longman

INDIVIDUAL TRIGGER PICTURES — C18

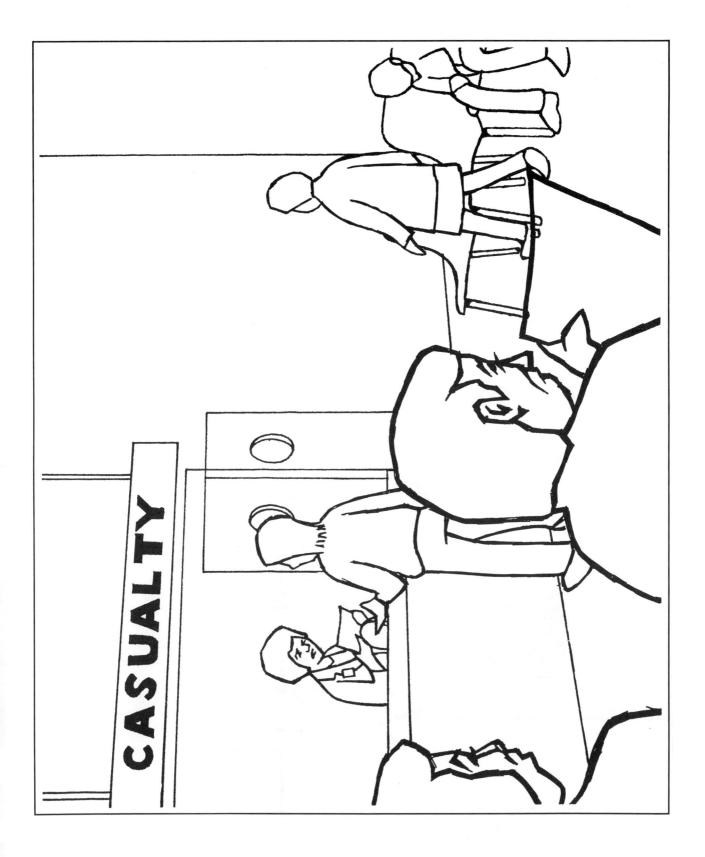

INDIVIDUAL TRIGGER PICTURES — C19

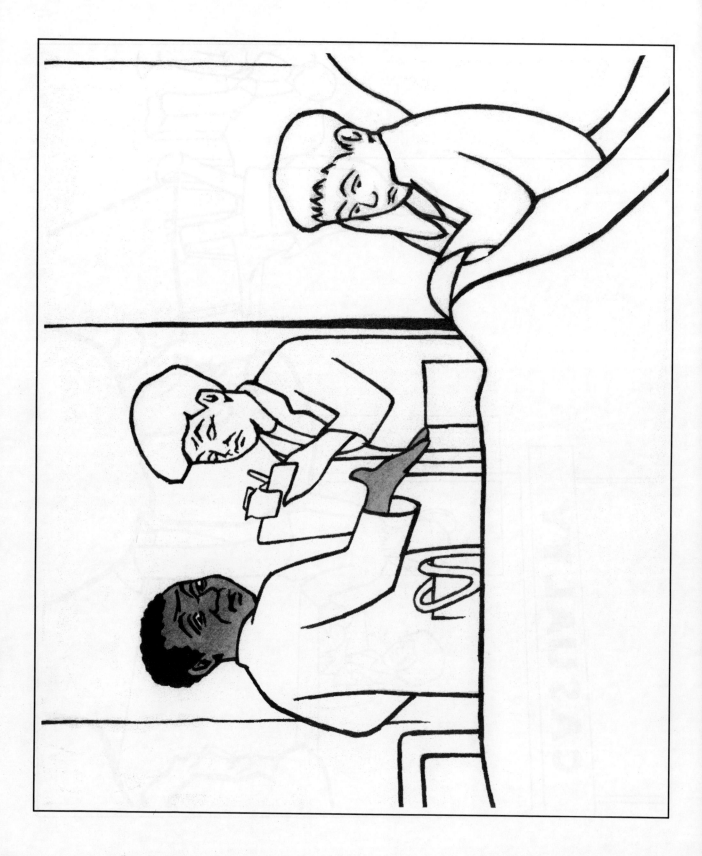

INDIVIDUAL TRIGGER PICTURES — C20

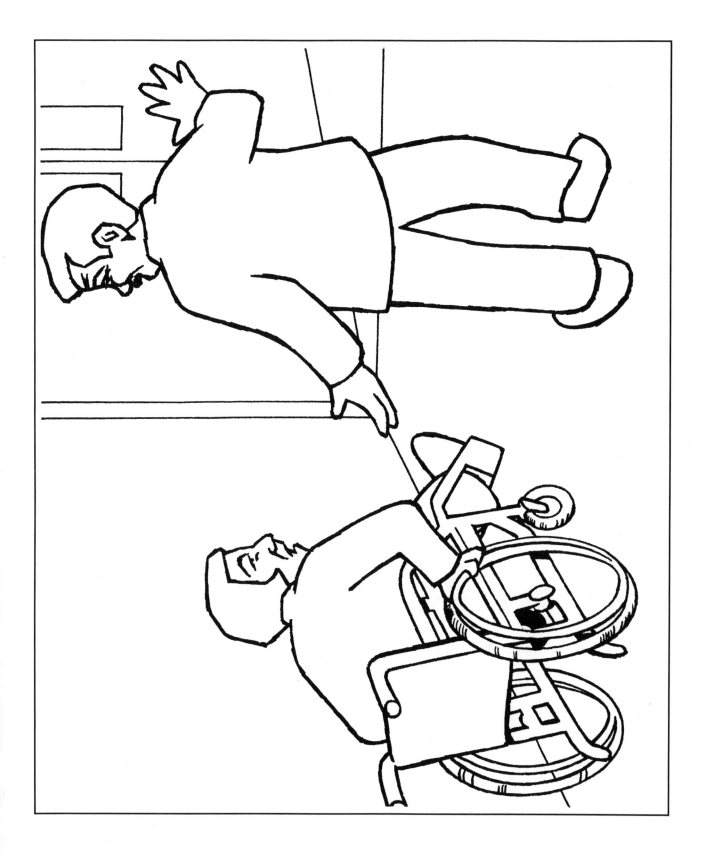

INDIVIDUAL TRIGGER PICTURES — C21

INDIVIDUAL TRIGGER PICTURES — C22

INDIVIDUAL TRIGGER PICTURES — C23

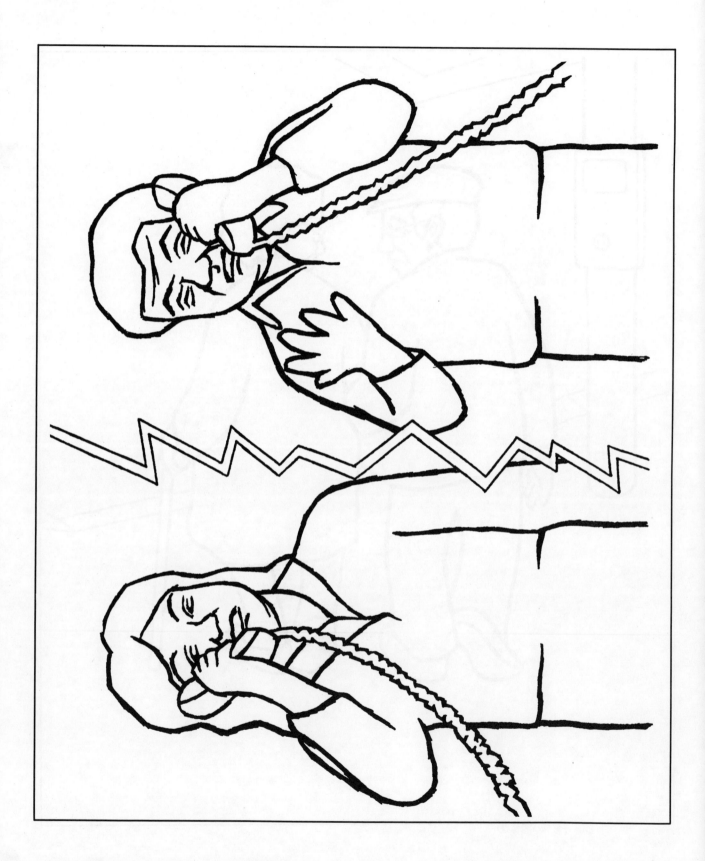

INDIVIDUAL TRIGGER PICTURES — C24

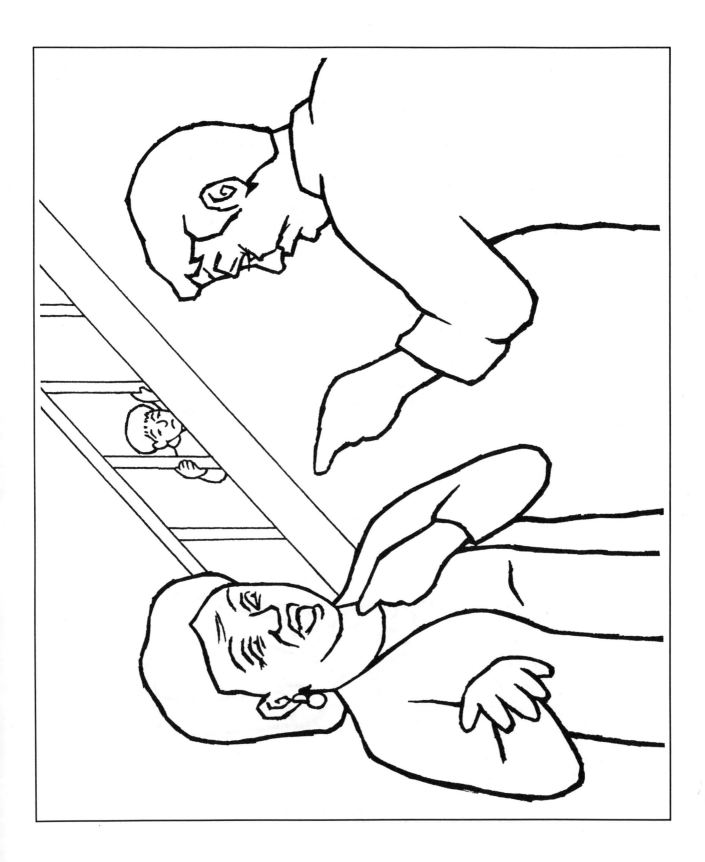

INDIVIDUAL TRIGGER PICTURES — C25

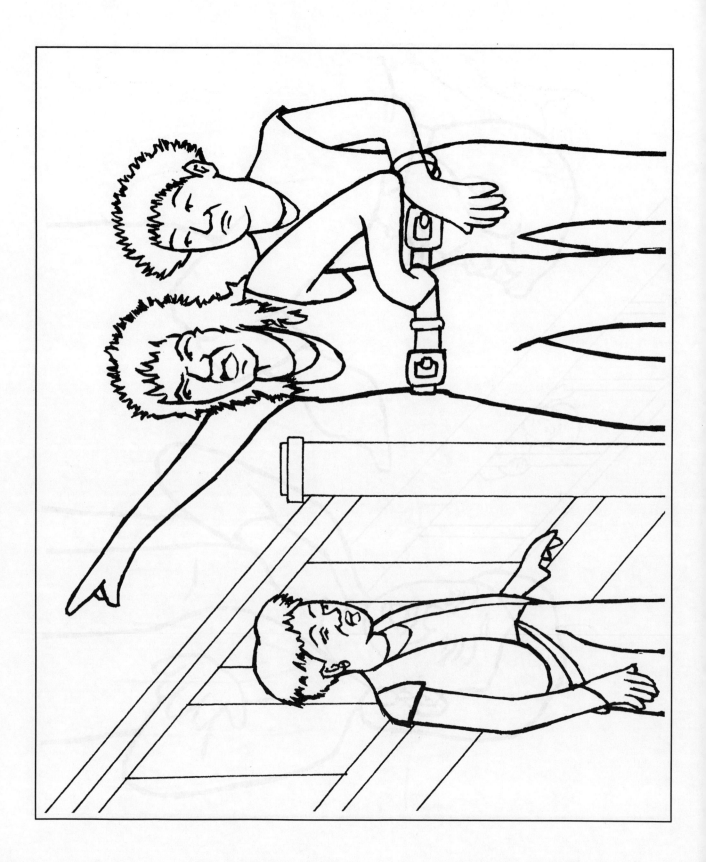

INDIVIDUAL TRIGGER PICTURES — C26

INDIVIDUAL TRIGGER PICTURES — C27

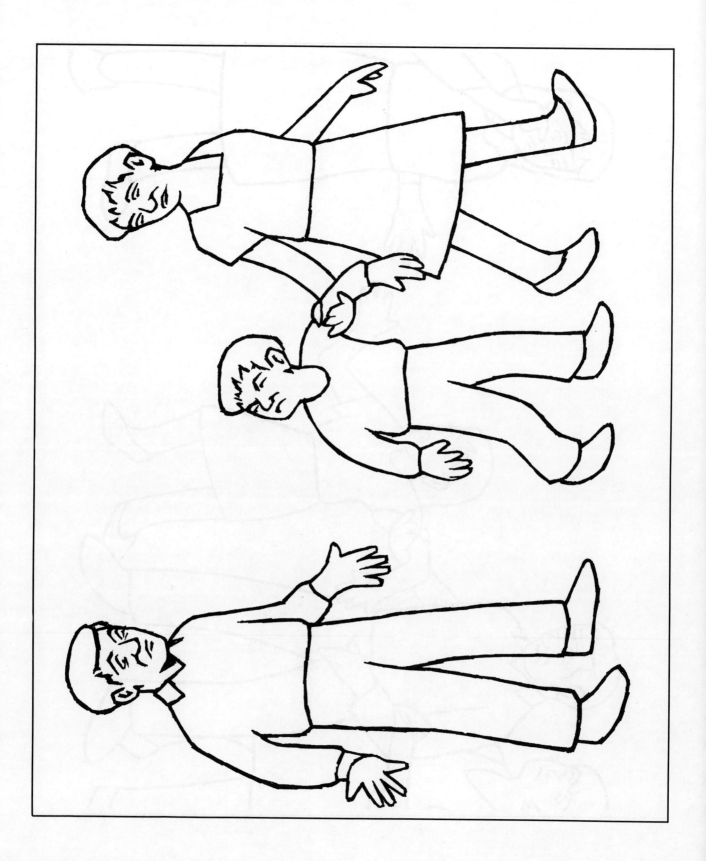

INDIVIDUAL TRIGGER PICTURES — C28

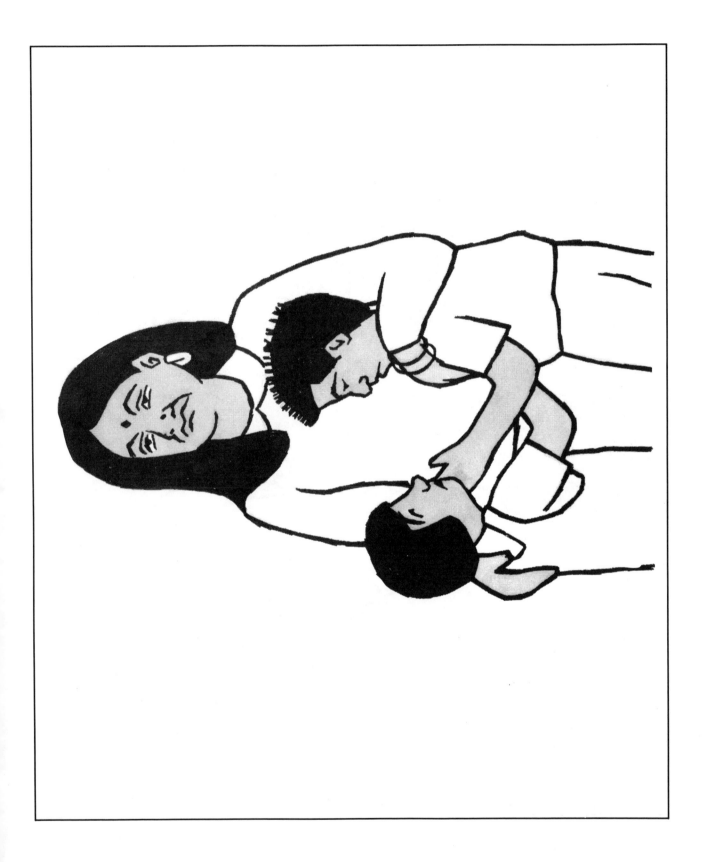

INDIVIDUAL TRIGGER PICTURES — C29

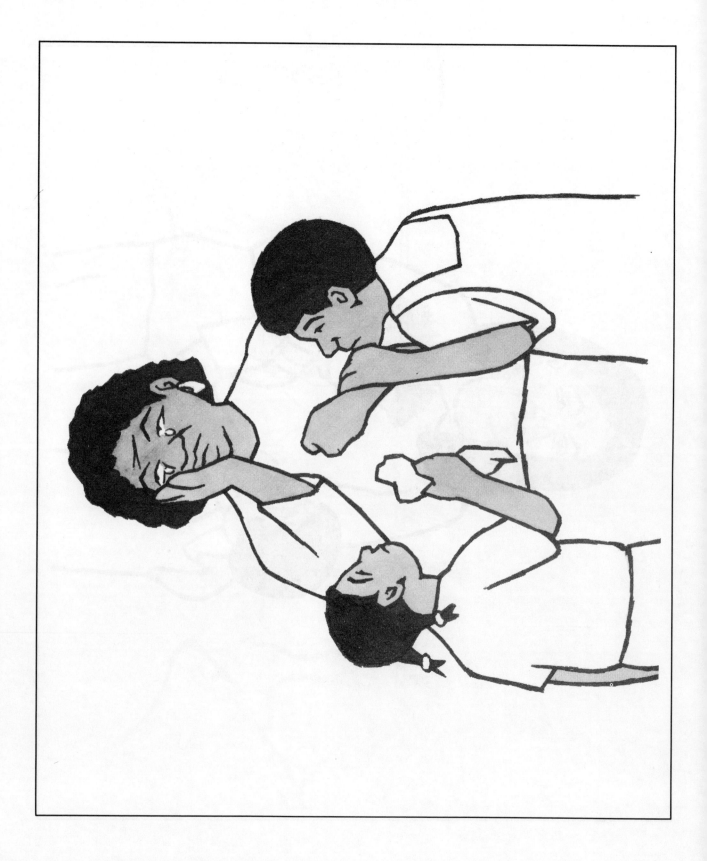

INDIVIDUAL TRIGGER PICTURES — C30

INDIVIDUAL TRIGGER PICTURES — C31

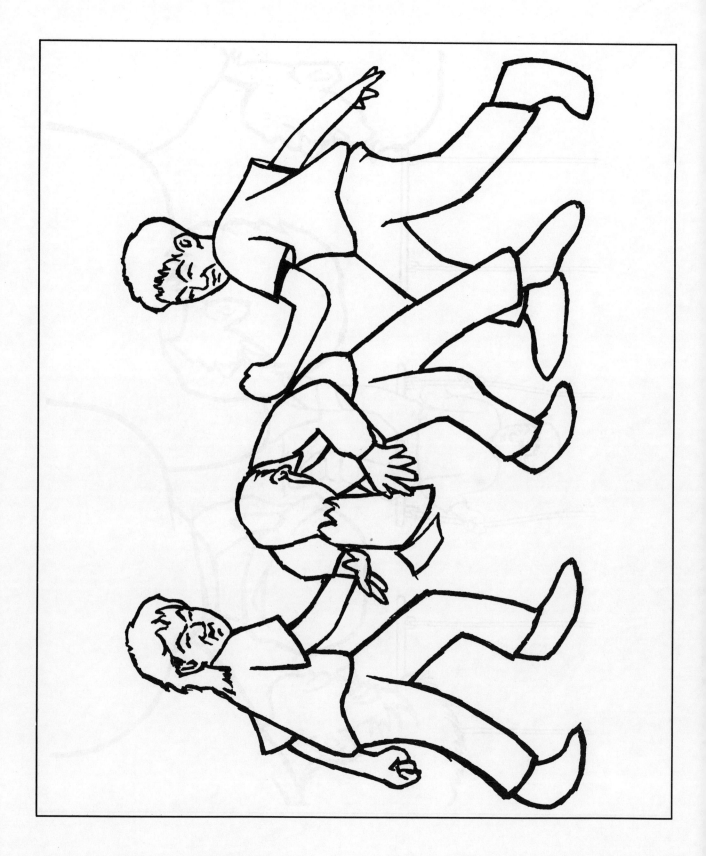

INDIVIDUAL TRIGGER PICTURES — C32

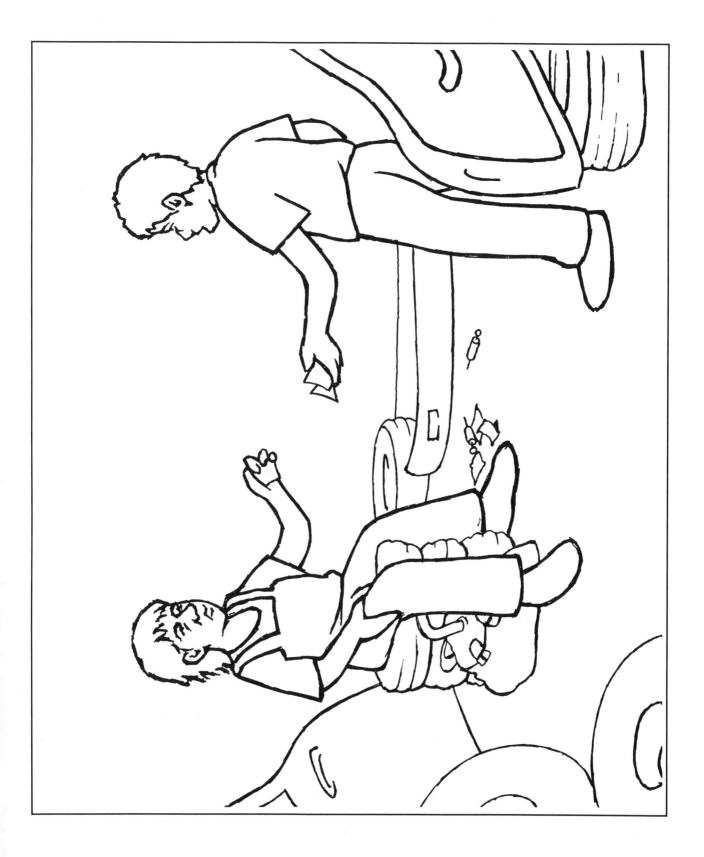

INDIVIDUAL TRIGGER PICTURES — C32

INDIVIDUAL TRIGGER PICTURES — C33

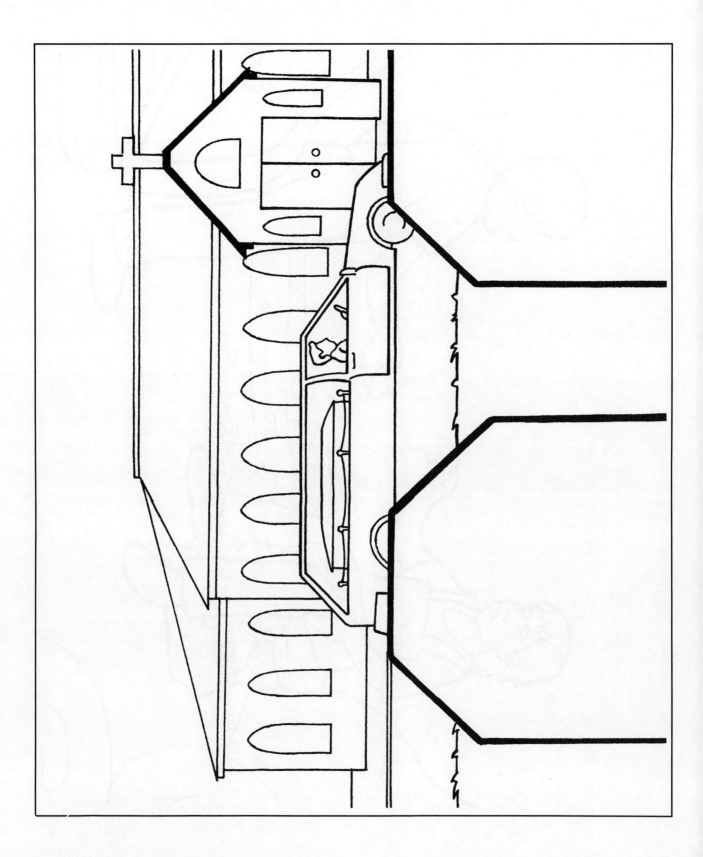

INDIVIDUAL TRIGGER PICTURES — C34

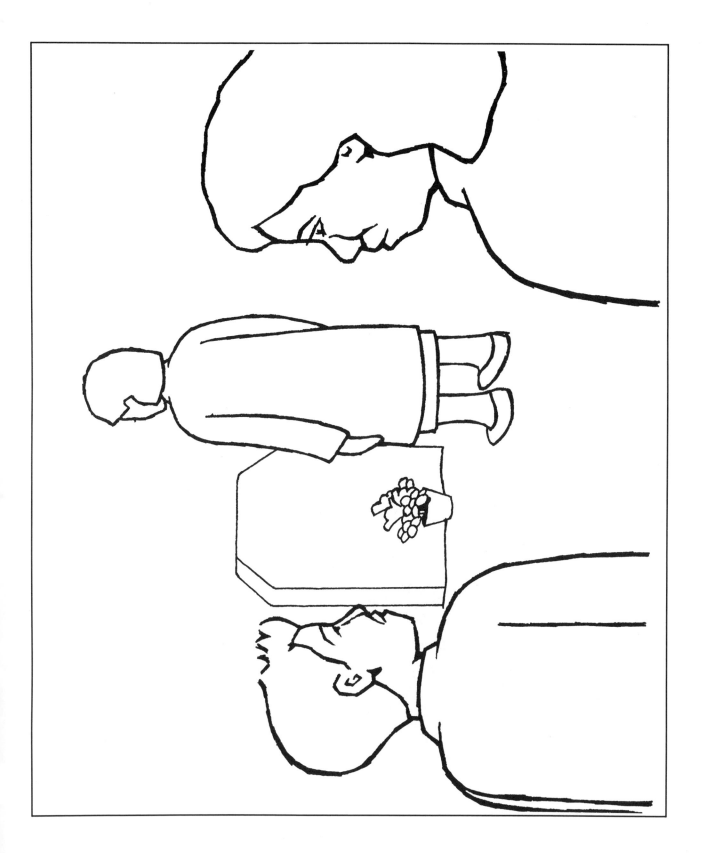

INDIVIDUAL TRIGGER PICTURES — C34

INDIVIDUAL TRIGGER PICTURES — C35

INDIVIDUAL TRIGGER PICTURES — C36

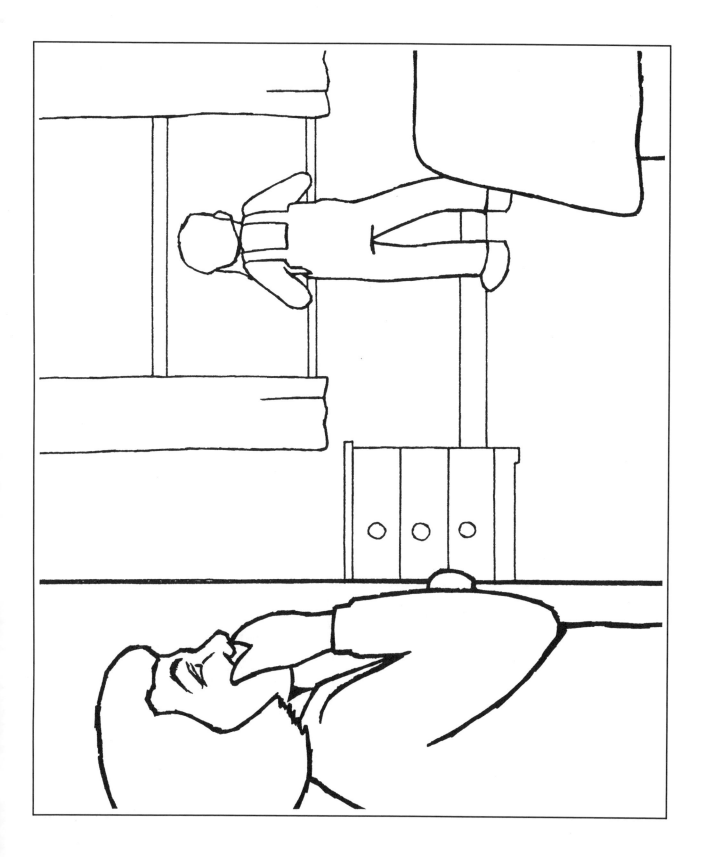

INDIVIDUAL TRIGGER PICTURES — C37

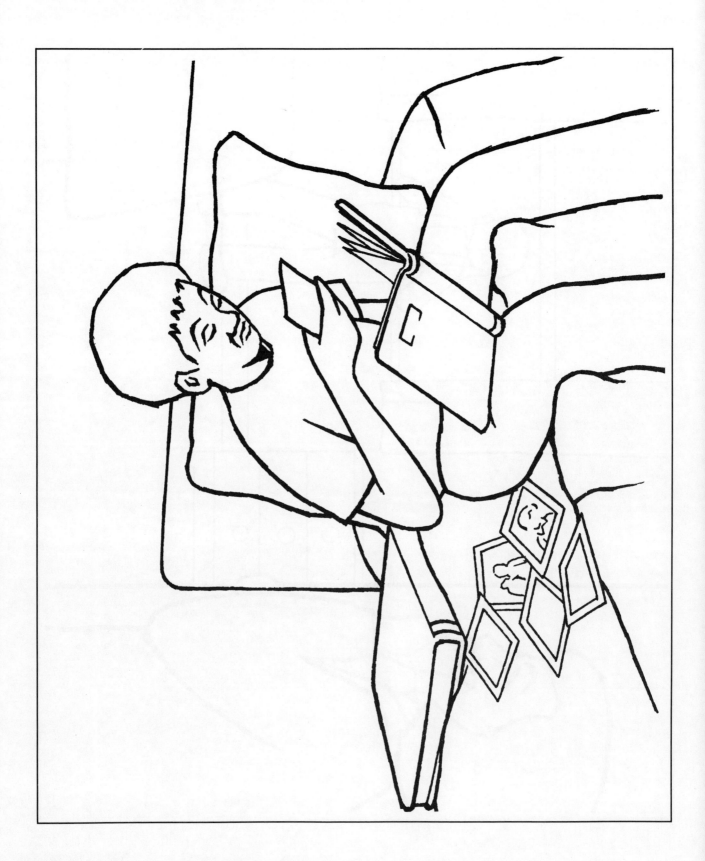

INDIVIDUAL TRIGGER PICTURES — C38

INDIVIDUAL TRIGGER PICTURES — C39

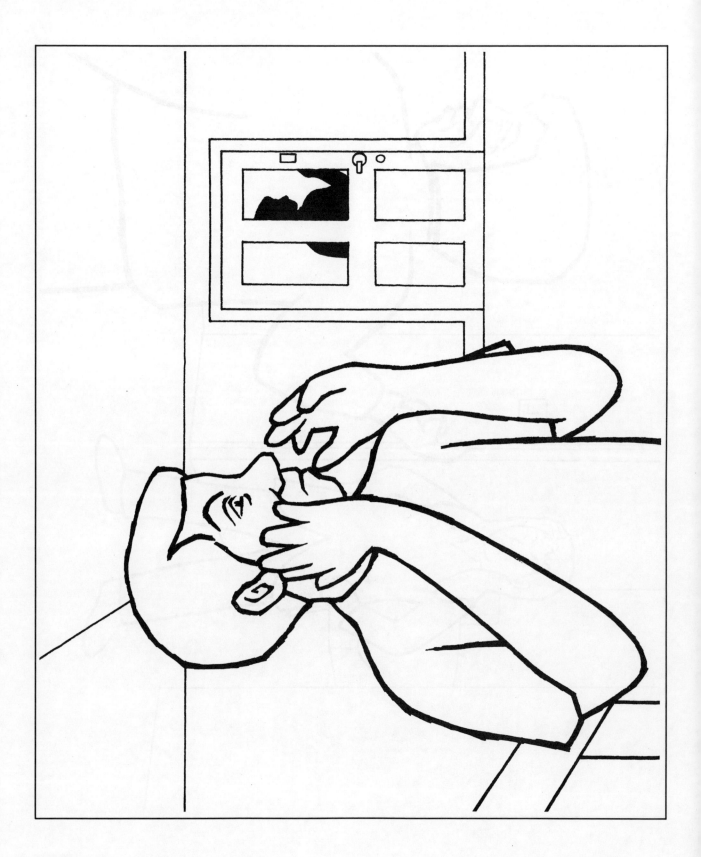

INDIVIDUAL TRIGGER PICTURES — C40

© Longman

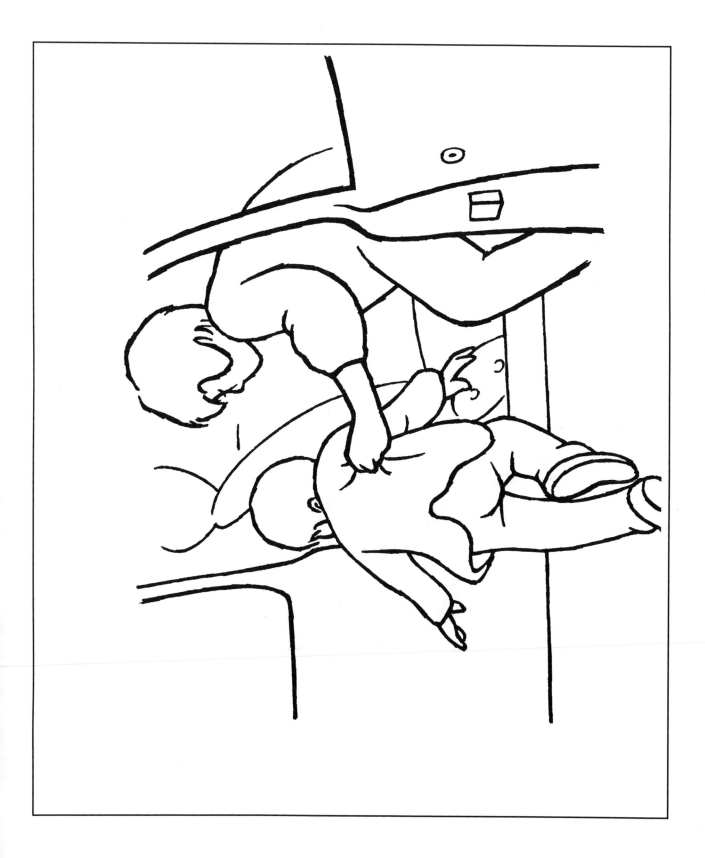

INDIVIDUAL TRIGGER PICTURES — C41

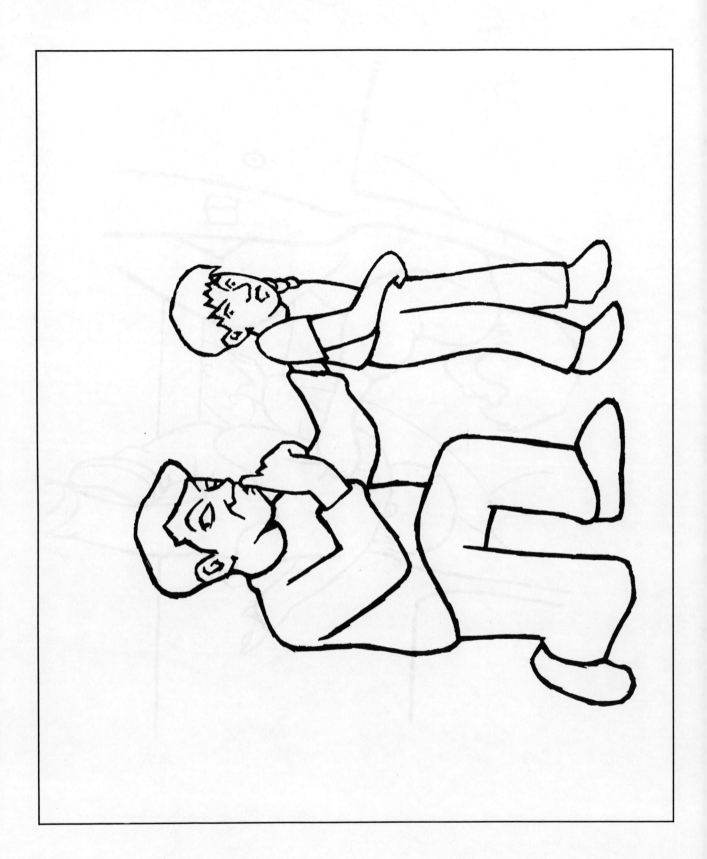

INDIVIDUAL TRIGGER PICTURES — C42

D — WORKSHEET 1

This is a picture of...

ME	A SPECIAL PERSON
SOMETHING SPECIAL	A SPECIAL PLACE

D — WORKSHEET 2

Draw a face which is ....

HAPPY	SAD
ANGRY	**AFRAID**

D — WORKSHEET 3

Here are some face shapes. Draw your own and your family (or friends or people you don't like). Write their name and something about them underneath, e.g. Ken makes me laugh, Katie is shy, etc.

D — WORKSHEET 4

Here are some face shapes. Draw your friends and some people you don't like. Write their names and something about them, e.g. Anne goes swimming with me, Tony hit me, etc.

D — WORKSHEET 5

These faces are partly drawn. Finish them by filling in the details of people they remind you of, e.g. Sally at the supermarket, Mr Dean the lollipop man, etc. Colour their faces and give them hair and, if you would like to, draw the kind of shirt or jumper they would be wearing.

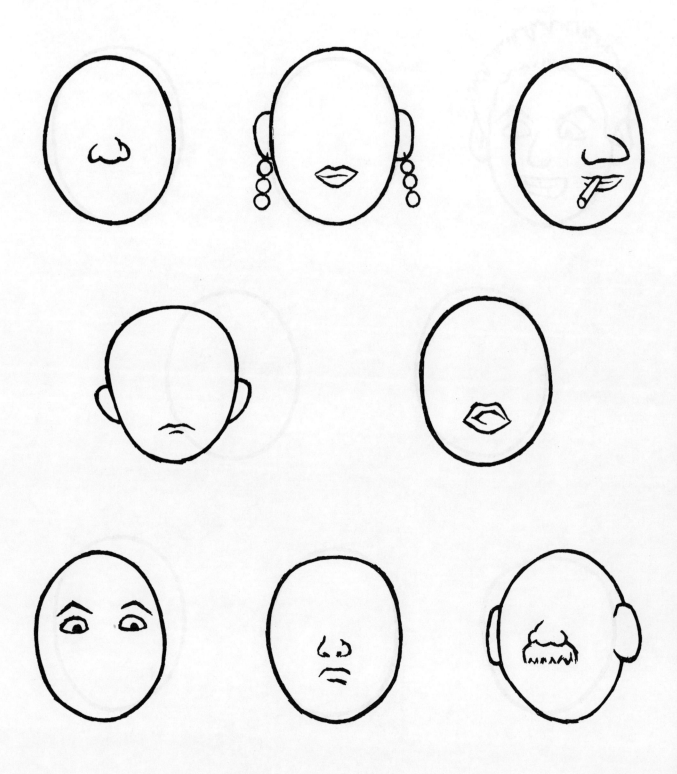

D — WORKSHEET 6

These faces are partly drawn. Finish them by filling in some happy and some scary people. Colour their faces and give them hair and, if you would like to, draw the kind of shirt or jumper they would be wearing.

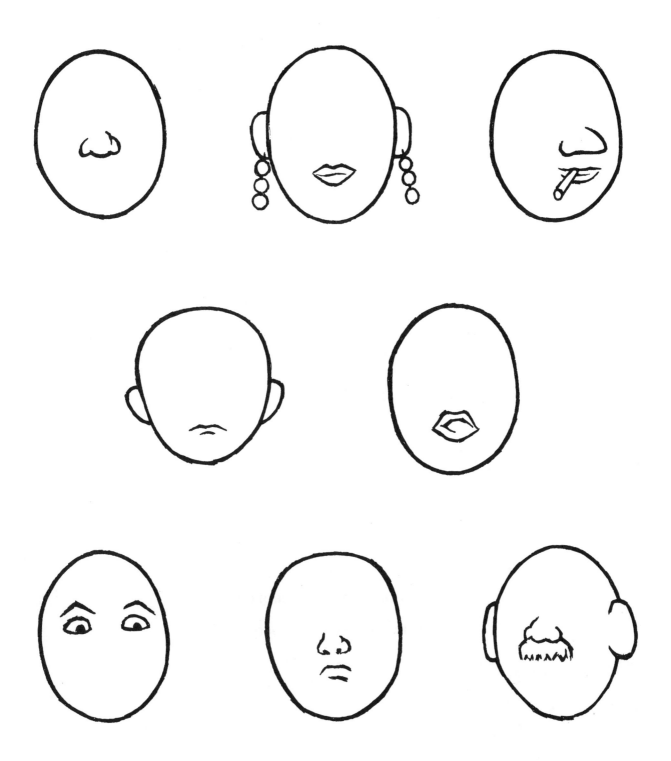

D — WORKSHEET 7

Draw yourself and other people on the picture.

What is happening in the picture?

What do you like about school?

What do you dislike about school?

D — WORKSHEET 8

Draw yourself in the picture, on the swing or walking in the park.

What are you doing in the park?

What are you thinking about in the park?

Do you like to be alone or with friends when you are in the park?

What does it feel like when you are alone? —
lonely/peaceful/quiet/left out/rejected/happy/sad.
(Underline any word that says how you feel when you are alone and add some more of
your own.)

What does it feel like when you are with friends?
happy/anxious/excited/adventurous/carefree/frightened.
(Underline any word that says how you feel when you are with friends and add some more
of your own.)

D – WORKSHEET 9

Draw yourself and anyone else you would like to put in the picture.

What are you, and the other people doing in the picture?

It is a happy or sad picture?

What might you be watching on television?

What is your favourite TV programme?

D — WORKSHEET 10

Draw yourself in the outline person on the picture. What is the expression on the face? What kind of clothes are you wearing?

Is this a happy picture or is it sad?

Write a story to go with the picture that is either happy or sad.

D — WORKSHEET 11

Draw a picture or write a story.

I AM FRIGHTENED WHEN . . .

D — WORKSHEET 12

Draw a picture or write a story . . .

MY BEST WISH IS . . .

D — WORKSHEET 13

Draw a picture or write a story.

I CRIED WHEN . . .

D — WORKSHEET 14

Draw a picture or write a story.

I WAS ANGRY WHEN . . .

D — WORKSHEET 15

Draw a picture or write a story.

MY HAPPIEST DAY WAS . . .

D — WORKSHEET 16

Draw a picture or write a story.

I LOVE . . .

D — WORKSHEET 17

Look at each of the pictures and say (or write down)

1.   What you think might be happening to the person.
2.   What they might be thinking.
3.   What they might be feeling.

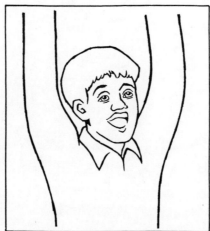
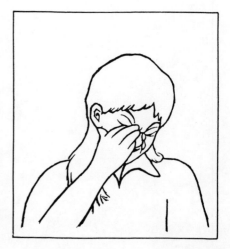

D — WORKSHEET 18

What do you think of when you look at each of these pictures?

What might the hands be doing or ''saying''.

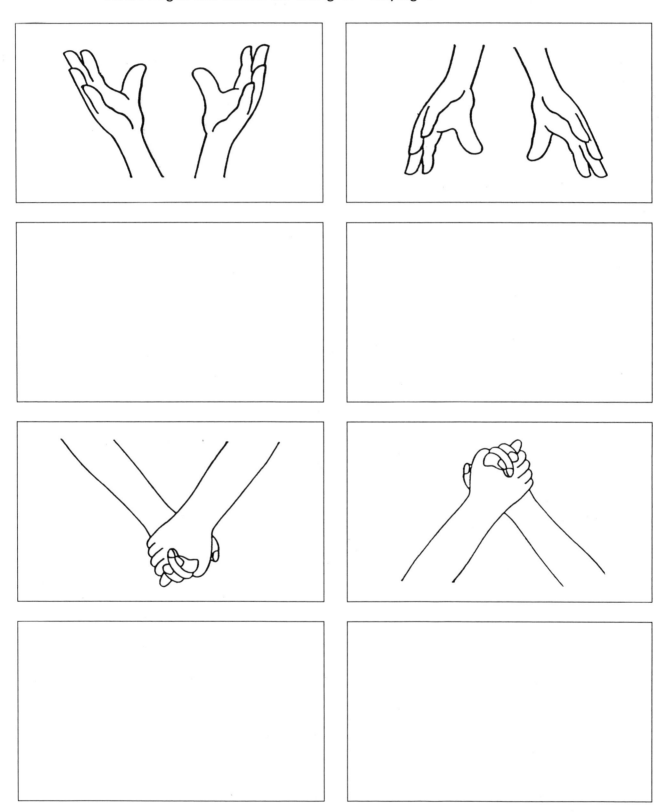

D — WORKSHEET 19

Look at each of the pictures and say (or write down) —

    1.   A good use for the object.

    2.   A bad use for the object.

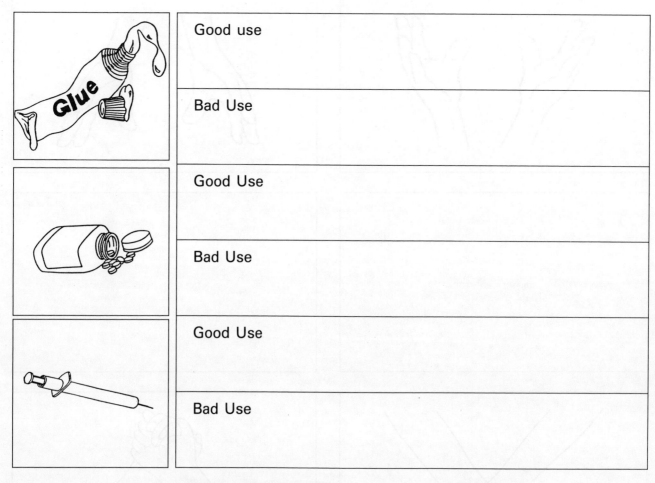

	Good use
	Bad Use
	Good Use
	Bad Use
	Good Use
	Bad Use

Write a story about one of these objects.

Once there was a . . .

D — WORKSHEET 20

Tell or write a happy and a sad story to go with each of these pictures.

A happy story

A sad story

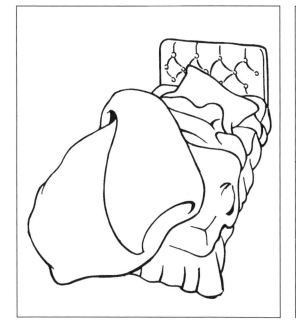

A happy story

A sad story

D — WORKSHEET 21

Tell or write a story about each of the pictures.

1. Think about a time before the picture and what life might have been like for the people.

2. Think about the reasons for a torn picture and a wheelchair.

3. Think about what might be happening now.

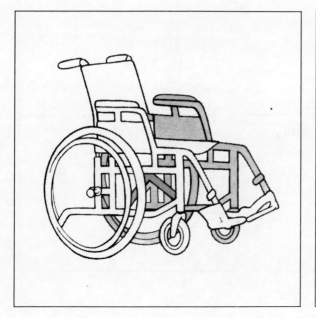

D — WORKSHEET 22

Talk or write about these pictures:

1. Say what feelings you have when you look at them.
2. What situation(s) do the pictures remind you of?

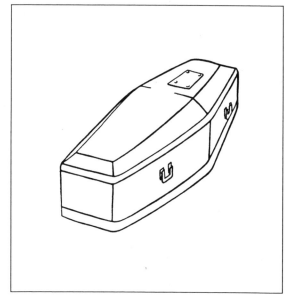

D — WORKSHEET 23

Tell or write a story about someone going away or dying.

D — WORKSHEET 24

Draw yourself on this picture and, if you wish, colour it in.

Write down what you think might be happening in the picture.

What is your favourite food?

Write down when you had a good meal time, e.g. a party, visiting friends, a wedding, etc.

Write down an occasion when you had a bad meal time, e.g. when there was an argument, you didn't like the food, someone was going to go away, etc.

D — WORKSHEET 25

Draw yourself and other people on the picture.

˙ What are you doing at the hospital?

What might you see at a hospital?

What might you hear at a hospital?

What might you smell at a hospital?

How do you feel when you go to the hospital?

D — WORKSHEET 26

Draw yourself in the outline person who is in bed. What expression do you want to put on the face? Colour your favourite nightie or pyjamas.

What are you feeling?

What might happen next? Tell the story of what follows from this scene.

D — WORKSHEET 27

Draw yourself in the outline person on the swing. What expression is on the face? Colour your favourite clothes.

Tell the story of what happens next with a happy ending.

Tell the story of what happens next with a sad ending.

D — WORKSHEET 28

Draw yourself in the outline person on the picture. What is the expression on the face? Colour your favourite clothes.

What is the grown-up saying?

What is the grown-up doing?

What would you like to happen next?

D — WORKSHEET 29

This castle has towers and dungeons. Sometimes it was used to keep people safe from dangers outside, at others it was used to lock people away so that they could do no harm. Draw your own castle and include the things and people you want to keep safe and those which you would like to be locked away.

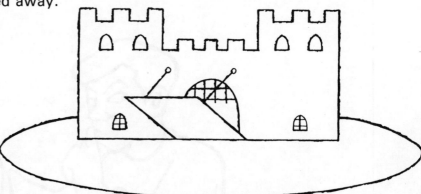

D — WORKSHEET 30

Write a story or draw a picture to show the BEST HELP that can be given to an unhappy child.

D — WORKSHEET 31

Draw a picture of a monster.

Is this a friendly monster who would help you or is it one that scares you?

What might this monster do?

D — WORKSHEET 32

Let your pen or pencil go all over the page and fill it with squiggles. When you have finished look for all the objects, people, and animals you can see in the shapes you have made.

D — WORKSHEET 33

Use any of the pictures from Section C. as a basis for a writing or drawing exercise.

Write a story about the picture OR

draw another picture to show what happened next.

D — WORKSHEET 34

Use the squares to tell a story of something important which has happened to you. It might be something happy and it might be something sad. (Or you could use photographs.)

1.

2.

3.

4.

5.

6.

D — WORKSHEET 35

Make a scrap book of the story of your life.

You may want to write or draw or use photographs or special cards you have received.

1. Describe yourself — how you look (perhaps use a photograph)
    - what you like
    - what you don't like
    - family
    - friends
    - other special people
    - pets

2. Describe important events
    - when you were born
    - early years
    - starting school
    - moving house
    - moving school
    - gaining new family members
    - losing family members
    - special days, birthdays, Christmas, etc.
    - being ill

This will take quite a lot of time so it is important to keep the papers and pictures and photographs safe because all of these things are about the special person which is ''you''. You may want to get a note book or scrap book to keep everything together.

Use this worksheet page as a check list and you could use it as an index on the first page.

SUGGESTED PROGRAMMES OF WORK USING THE PICTURES

These suggestions are only intended to give general guidelines which are not a substitute for the carer/counsellor thoughtfully deciding a work programme to suit the particular needs of an individual or a group.

Bereavement

- A 1. getting lost
- 2. losing a gift
- 3. death of a pet
- B 6. illness
- C 17. ambulance
- 23. telephone
- 33. church
- 34. grave
- 29. tears
- 37. photographs
- D worksheets — 1, 2, 3, 8, 13, 17, 22, 23, 30, 34, 35.

Illness and disability

- A 4. illness
- B 6. illness
- C 18. casualty
- 20. wheelchair
- 11. wheelchair in a race
- D worksheets — 1, 2, 5, 6, 8, 12, 13, 14, 17, 19, 21, 25, 26, 31, 32.

Damaged relationships

- A 5. moving to another ''home''
- B 8. relationships
- C 24. a quarrel
- 26. people in conflict
- 23. telephone
- 28. group sadness
- 35. waiting
- D worksheets — 1, 2, 3, 4, 6, 9, 11, 12, 16, 18, 20, 21, 24, 29, 30, 31, 34.

Working to such a programme will take a number of sessions to be completed. The age of the child, and the length of the session will clearly also contribute to the pacing of the work.

SUGGESTED PROGRAMMES OF WORK USING THE PICTURES

These suggestions are only intended to give general guidelines which are not a substitute for the care counsellor thoughtfully deciding a work programme to suit the particular needs of an individual or a group.

Bereavement

- A 1. getting lost
-   2. losing a pet
-   3. death of a per...
- B 6. illness
- C 7. ambulance
-   23. telephone
-   33. church
-   34. grave...
-   22. tears
-   37. photographs
- D worksheets — 1, 2, 3, 8, 13, 17, 22, 23, 30, 34, 35.

Illness and disability

- A 4. illness
- B 5. illness
- C 16. casualty
-   ... wheelchair
-   11. wheelchair in a park
- D worksheets — 1, 2, 5, 6, 9, 12, 13, 14, 17, 18, 21, 25, 29, 31, 32.

Damaged relationships

- A 5. moving to another home
- B 8. relationships
-   ... a party
-   20. people in conflict
-   22. telephone
-   28. group sadness
-   35. waiting
- D worksheets — 1, 2, 3, 4, 5, 11, 12, 18, 19, 20, 24, 28, 30, 31, 33.

Working in such a programme will likely run a number of sessions to be completed. The number of sessions and the length of these sessions will depend very much upon the needs of the young ...